PUFFIN BOOKS

DARE TO ASK YOURSELF

Kate Tym has dared to ask herself several important questions and has found out the following …

Kate has written numerous books for children, both fiction and non-fiction. When she's not writing, she wears an editor's hat and tells other people what to write instead. Kate lives in North London with her cat, Muffy.

Kate Tym

DARE TO ASK YOURSELF

PUFFIN BOOKS

PUFFIN BOOKS

Published by the Penguin Group
Penguin Books Ltd, 27 Wrights Lane, London W8 5TZ, England
Penguin Putnam Inc., 375 Hudson Street, New York, New York 10014, USA
Penguin Books Australia Ltd, Ringwood, Victoria, Australia
Penguin Books Canada Ltd, 10 Alcorn Avenue, Toronto, Ontario, Canada M4V 3B2
Penguin Books (NZ) Ltd, Private Bag 102902, NSMC, Auckland, New Zealand

On the World Wide Web at: www.penguin.com

Penguin Books Ltd, Registered Offices: Harmondsworth, Middlesex, England

First published 2000
1 3 5 7 9 10 8 6 4 2

The moral right of the author has been asserted
Designed by Tony Fleetwood

Set in Kabel Book 11/13pt

Made and printed in England by Clays Ltd, St Ives plc

British Library Cataloguing in Publication Data
A CIP catalogue record for this book is available from the British Library

ISBN 0–141–30505–3

Contents

Introduction

Me, myself, I ...

So you think you know yourself pretty well, do you? Well, we'll see about that. By the time you've finished this book you really *will* know yourself – inside out, back to front and top to toe! No aspect of your personality will be left unexamined and you'll be amazed at just what will be revealed. From an amazing new self-awareness to understanding your best buddy and even finding out how other people see you, you'll soon be totally clued up about everything that makes you tick!

Before You Start

Before you start, make sure you've got all the equipment you'll need to do the job properly. Yep, that's right, you're going to have to make a bit of an investment and get yourself some paper, or a notebook, and a pen. (How you reacted to that might have told you something about yourself already!)

Now, the notes you make on your paper or in your notebook are going to be Top Secret, so keep them somewhere safe. After all, you don't want just anybody finding out everything there is to know about you, do you? Once you've got the equipment you need, there'll be no stopping you. So start turning the pages and finding out **All About You!**

Personality Profile

Throughout this book you'll find **key words** listed underneath each of the quiz results. Make sure you note down every key word you get as you complete the quizzes. This way, at the end of the book you will have a list of words that show all the different sides of your character – your total personality profile! Some of the words may seem to contradict each other, but that's the crazy thing about being human. Just because you're a total science boffin doesn't mean you

can't like arty things too, and being a bit indecisive sometimes doesn't mean that you can't be really grounded and sure of yourself at others. Life's just like that! But it's also what makes you special. So what are you waiting for? With pen and paper at the ready, it's time to get going!

THE
REAL
ME

All About Me

Why not begin by using your first page to write down a few personal details – an initial profile? Here are some ideas to get you started:

Name	Birthday
Age	Sisters
Eye colour	Brothers
Hair colour	Star sign
Height	Pets
Weight	Best friend
Parents' names	

Then, how about listing some of your favourite things?

Fave singer	Fave soap
Fave band	Fave film
Fave shop	Fave girl's name
Fave actress	Fave boy's name
Fave actor	Fave subject
Fave food	Fave colour

And how about some personal stuff?

The most exciting thing I've ever done is …

My top tip for a rainy day is …

The best thing that has ever happened to me is …

The worst thing that has ever happened to me is …

The best book I've ever read is …

The best film I've ever seen is …

I collect …

Finally, the reason for keeping your notebook well hidden, your top ten secrets!

I bet you've found out quite a lot about yourself already!

Cool in a Crisis

or a MESS UNDER STRESS?

When you're having a seriously bad day, do you keep your head or fall apart at the seams? Basically, are you a cucumber or a jelly? Now's the time to find out!

1 It's day one at your new school. You've had to go and see the headmaster first thing, so you're a bit late for registration. You dash to your classroom, burst through the door, trip over your bag strap and fall flat on your face in front of the whole class. Do you:

A. Stand up, dust yourself down and take a bow in front of your laughing classmates – you certainly know how to break the ice?

B. Crawl towards the door without looking up, shoot straight out of it and then run down the corridor, red-faced and crying?

C. Pick yourself up off the floor, then stammer something incomprehensible and take your seat, trying to act as if it never even happened?

2 You're baby-sitting your little sister for ten minutes while your mother's gone to the shops. Little sis falls, cuts her knee and starts bawling her head off. Her knee's bleeding, but it doesn't look too bad. Do you:

A. Drag your screaming sister round to the neighbours – they'll know what to do?

B. Call an ambulance in hysterics – it might be worse than it looks?

C. Soothe your sister and dry her tears, then wash the cut, put a plaster on it and give her a big kiss better – and all before your mother gets home?

3 You've got a school test coming up and you know deep down that you haven't really done enough work for it. When the day dawns, do you:

A. By some strange coincidence start feeling incredibly ill? Maybe you can be excused the test today and sit it next week, by which time you'll know a bit more!

B. Get so nervous in the test that you forget how to read English and go completely blank?

C. Accept the fact that it's too late to change anything now and just concentrate on doing the best you can?

4 You're talking with your friend about a girl in your class who's wearing some really naff hair-slides. Suddenly she appears in front of you. She's been listening to the whole thing! Do you say:

A. 'Fooled you! You thought I didn't know you were there, didn't you? Of course I did. Why do you think I was saying all that

rubbish about your hair-slides? They're really nice by the way!'?
B. 'Oh, hi! That's, er, really funny … We were just talking about this other girl with the same name as you who's got these really horrible slides in her hair. Not you, of course. I mean, I wouldn't talk about you. I mean, your slides are lovely …' while going bright red?
C. 'Oh, no! You heard everything I said, didn't you?', bury your face in your hands and run away?

5 **At the end of term everyone in your class has to stand up and talk for five minutes on a subject of their choice. When it's your turn, do you:**
A. Go hot and cold, have heart palpitations and mumble and fumble your way through a five-minute period that seems to last for five hours?
B. Say, 'Miss, I didn't know anything about it. I must have been away that day. I, er … What do you mean I'll have to improvise!!!'?
C. Stand up, take a deep breath and do your best to make a good job of it – that's all anyone can ask of you, surely?

6 **You've been walking around with your skirt tucked in the back of your knickers for about half an hour. When someone points it out to you, do you:**
A. Coolly say, 'Oh, didn't you realize it's the latest look?' and pretend you're not really bothered?
B. Tug your skirt out of your pants and, when someone mentions it later, say, 'It wasn't me. It was just someone who looks like me!'?
C. Tug your skirt out of your pants, burst into tears and run?

7 **You've just started at a new school. A girl in your class invites you to her birthday party, which is on the Saturday at the end of your first week. Do you:**
A. Buy her a present and a card, put on your favourite outfit and get on over to her house? It was nice of her to ask you and you're

not missing out on the ideal opportunity to get to know the other people in your class.

B. Buy her a present (then worry she won't like it), put on your favourite outfit (then worry you'll look out of place) and spend the whole party feeling nervous, tongue-tied and worrying you don't fit in? You have such an awful time that you can hardly wait for your mum to come and pick you up to take you home again.

C. Say, 'Forget it!'? There's no way you're going to a party full of people you don't really know.

Now add up your scores:

1. A.15 B.5 C.10   2. A.10 B.5 C.15   3. A.10 B.5 C.15

4. A.15 B.10 C.5   5. A.5 B.10 C.15   6. A.15 B.10 C.5

7. A. 15 B. 10 C. 5

86–105 Ice Cool

Nothing fazes you, does it? You're so calm it's not true. You can handle any situation standing on your head and simply refuse to be ruffled. On the whole, this is a great way to be. You can make yourself do things that would leave most people quivering in the corner like a land-locked jellyfish. But remember, it's OK to find some things daunting – you're only human, after all. You don't need to be ashamed if you have to ask for help from time to time. In fact, if you admit to others that some things do give you the heebie-jeebies, they might find you just a little less daunting!

Key word: solid

56–85 Living in Denial

Well, your coping strategy is pretty transparent: you just pretend

whatever it is isn't really happening in the vain hope that it'll just go away and everything will turn out to have been a nasty dream all along! Sometimes you can pull off this bluffer's approach, but most of the time I'm afraid that you can't. You're going to have to learn to take responsibility for yourself. But remember, if something scares you, there's nothing wrong with asking for a bit of help. You'll be amazed to find out that if you face up to your fears, things are often not as bad as you think! And the more often you do it, the easier it gets!

Key words: in denial

35–55 No Coper

Oh dear, oh dear. If things aren't going your way you cry or run! It's probably not the ideal way to deal with situations that frighten you. Remember, *everyone* gets scared or fearful at one time or another – you're not the only one. When you're next in a potential panic, take a deep breath and count to ten before doing anything. If you approach things calmly, you may well find they're not nearly as bad as you thought they were anyway. Good luck. I'm sure the new super-cool you is just dying to shine through!

Key word: anxious

Animal Magic

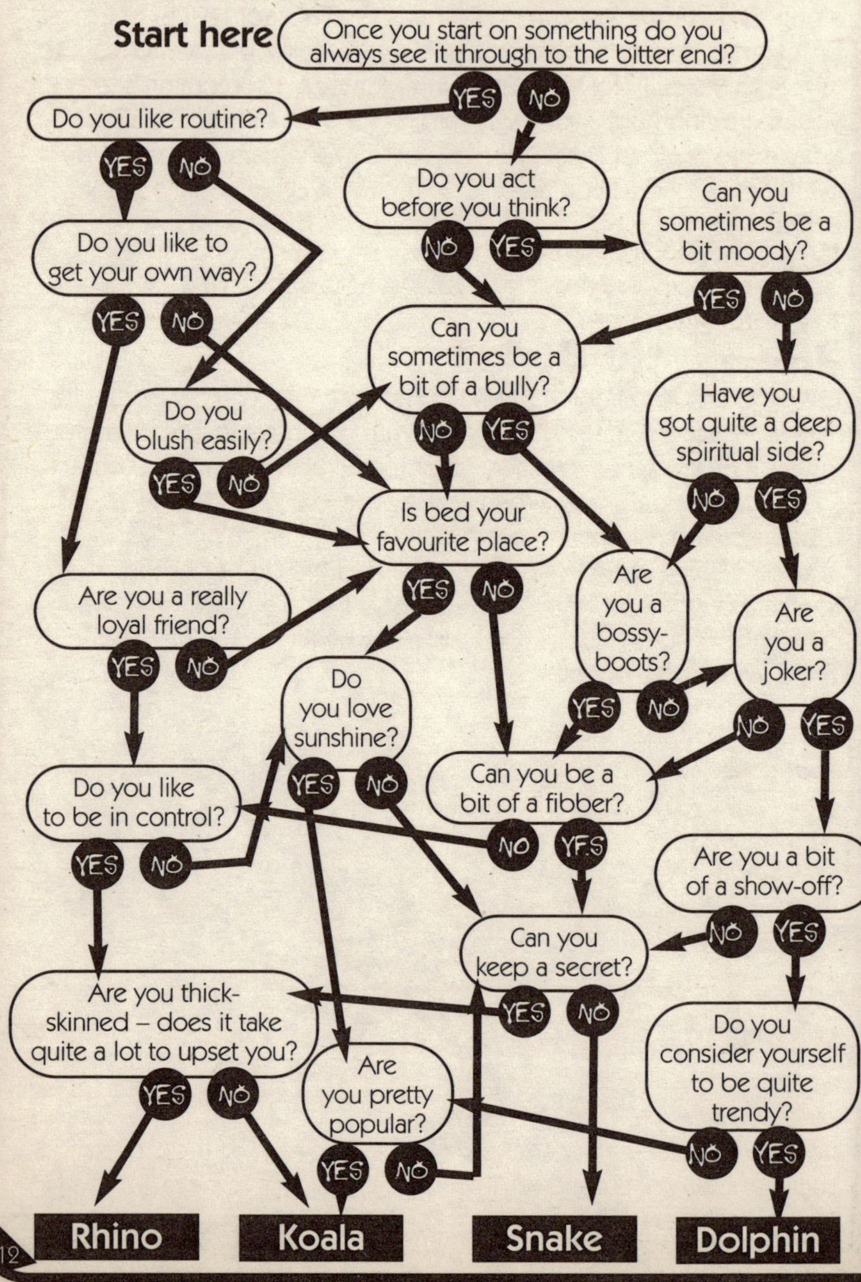

If you were transformed into any creature on the whole teeming planet, what would you be? Check it out …

You're a … Wrinkly Rhino

Ah! Like the wrinkly rhino of the hot African plains, you just don't like to be told what to do. You've got your own way of doing things and that's how you want it to stay. Having said that, your heart's definitely in the right place and, as a friend, you are as loyal as they come, because once you've made up your mind about something, there isn't any way you're changing it … ever! Just try to remember that a little flexibility is not a bad thing.

Key word: stubborn

You're a … Cutie Koala

What a fluffy little softie you are! You're a bit of a dozy one and prefer to let others make the decisions for you. You can be a bit on the shy side and might have to learn to stand up for yourself every now and again. The good thing about you is that, like a cuddly koala, you're pretty hard to resist, so popularity won't ever be a problem where you're concerned.

Key word: shy

You're a … Dreamy Dolphin

You're quite a with-it chick. You're kind, caring, intelligent and popular. You like a laugh, you're energetic and it's often hard to tell what you're going to do next. But you balance all this with a sensitive side and your concern for the environment. You're also a good organizer and like a challenge – wow, what an all-round star you are!

Key word: energetic

You're a … Slippery Snake

Oh dear, you're not being very nice at the moment, are you? You can be a bit of an old bossy-boots, you're mad on gossip and you tend to find it pretty hard to keep a secret! Not always the best way to hang on to your chums! So, sort your snaky self out and you'll soon be as hissing fit as the next critter!

Key word: bossy

Dress It Up ★

Are you a disco diva or a hippie chick? Find out what your clothes are saying about you in this clever clothing quiz!
In each of the columns below, four items of clothing are listed (labelled A, B, C and D). Pick one item of clothing from each of the numbered columns, making sure that the combination you choose contains one of each of the letters (i.e. A, B, C and D). Then read the conclusions below to see what the combination you chose says about you!

1	2	3	4
A. Tiara	A. Trendy glasses	A. Hooded sweat top	A. Cloth drawstring bag
B. Suit jacket	B. T-shirt	B. White embroidered blouse	B. Feather boa
C. Long print skirt	C. Sparkly strappy dress	C. Suit skirt	C. Leggings
D. Trainers	D. Sandals	D. Strappy-heeled sandals	D. Trendy shoes

1A, 2C, 3D, 4B: Glam Girl

You're a disco diva, a party queen. You love anything that sparkles and you're very fond of silky-satiny materials and fluffy feathers. You're a natural-born performer and love being the centre of attention. When Hollywood calls, you want to look the part!

Key word: glam

1B, 2A, 3C, 4D: Power Dresser

You like to look smart and sharp. You're confident and ambitious, and you like your clothes to reflect that. You're a hard worker and are keen to get on, but you also like to be hip and keep a close eye on what's in.

Key word: smart

1C, 2D, 3B, 4A: Hippie Chick

Hey, man, you look really cool! You like floaty fabrics and flat shoes. You care about the environment and would love to travel and see the world.

Key word: hippie

1D, 2B, 3A, 4C: Sport-oholic

Wow! Do you like a workout or what? You're always on the go, so you need your clothes to be adaptable and flexible for everything you want to do. Either that or you just like to be comfy while you slob in front of the telly!

Key word: sporty

None of the above: Nancy Non-conformer

You've really got a mind of your own. You won't be dictated to by fashion or clothing rules – you'll wear what you like, how you like. You don't feel the need to follow the crowd. Instead, you prefer to set your own trends and let everyone else follow.

Key word: non-conformer

Worldly

Are you in the know about different places and cultures, or does everything that happens beyond your own front doorstep pass you by? Now's your chance to find out.

1. Where is the Taj Mahal?
A. India
B. Russia
C. America

2. Where's the Eiffel Tower?
A. The town of Eiffel, France
B. In Paris, France
C. In Sydney, Australia

Wise

3. Where do tigers live?
A. Africa
B. India
C. Egypt

4. Where do koalas live?
A. Australia
B. Bangladesh
C. Thailand

5. Who was Vincent Van Gogh?
A. A Dutch painter
B. A German writer
C. A French composer

6. Which country does the island of Crete belong to?
A. Turkey
B. Italy
C. Greece

7. Which country is Reykjavik the capital of?
A. Finland
B. Iceland
C. Sri Lanka

8. How do you say 'Goodbye' in German?
A. Sies du
B. Auf Wiedersehen
C. Bonjour

9. How do you say 'Goodbye' in French?
A. Au revoir
B. Guten Tag
C. Salute

10. Where are the Rocky Mountains?
A. South Africa
B. North America
C. Israel

11. Who was Claude Monet?
A. A French painter
B. A Spanish dancer
C. An Italian composer

12. Where does Flamenco dancing come from?
A. Afghanistan
B. Spain
C. Mozambique

13. How many languages can you say two words or more in?
A. None but my own language
B. Two or three
C. Four or more

14. When you visit new places/countries, do you feel:
A. Really, really excited?
B. Really, really worried?
C. Really, really bored?

15. If you get taken out for a meal, do you:
A. Always choose the thing on the menu you've eaten before?
B. Always try something new?
C. Try something new, then worry you won't like it?

16. Do you make new friends:
A. Always really easily?
B. Sometimes easily?
C. Not very easily?

#	A	B	C
1.	A.10	B.0	C.0
2.	A.0	B.10	C.0
3.	A.0	B.10	C.0
4.	A.10	B.0	C.0
5.	A.10	B.0	C.0
6.	A.0	B.0	C.10
7.	A.0	B.10	C.0
8.	A.0	B.10	C.0
9.	A.10	B.0	C.0
10.	A.0	B.10	C.0
11.	A.10	B.0	C.0
12.	A.0	B.10	C.0
13.	A.0	B.5	C.10
14.	A.10	B.5	C.0
15.	A.0	B.10	C.5
16.	A.10	B.5	C.0

130—160 Worldly Wise

What a fount of all knowledge you are! You're a real inquisitive type – the world you live in interests you and you like to find out all about it. You'd like to travel and try new things. There's a whole great big world out there and you just can't wait to start exploring. For the time being you might have to make do with books and travel programmes on the telly. But if you are lucky enough to have some time abroad, why not try to learn at least three phrases in the language

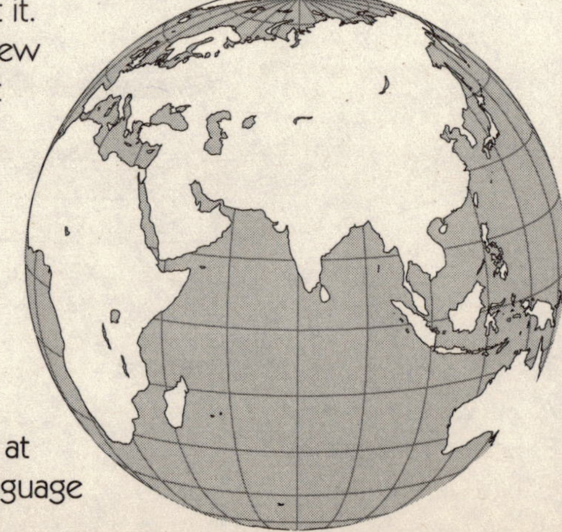

of that country and find
out three facts to impress
your family and friends with.
Soon you'll be able to say
'Good morning' to almost
anyone you meet!
Key word: adventurous

60–129
Worldly Wonder

Mmm, not bad – a couple of those
questions were pretty tricky! You are
quite keen to find out about the world you
live in, but sometimes feel a bit on edge in new situations. You are
interested in other countries, but you also quite like staying closer
to home. You'd like to start with countries where they speak the
same language as you before getting more adventurous later on.
You will try some new things, but you're always a bit nervous that
you might not like them. Don't worry … if you don't like something
you don't have to do it again. But you never know, if you try something new you might just find you absolutely love it!
Key word: conventional

0–59 World Weary

You're a bit of a Susie-stay-at-home. You like your home comforts
and can't really see the point of going through all the rigmarole of
planning and executing a major expedition when you've got everything you need right here. And that's OK if you never want to
expand your horizons beyond your four bedroom walls. But just
think of all the new and exciting things you could learn – and I
don't just mean about other people and places, I mean about
yourself too!
Key word: conservative

CONFIDENT OR NOT?

Confidence is a state of mind, and a little bit can go a long, long way. But be careful not to get too cocky or you could be heading for a fall. Try this three-part quiz to find out how much confidence you have.

STATE OF MIND

Do you ever have thoughts like the ones listed on the next page? Read each of the seven statements in turn and think about how much you agree with them. Then, using the scale 1–5, choose the answer you most agree with for each of the statements. Make a note of what you score for each statement on a piece of paper.

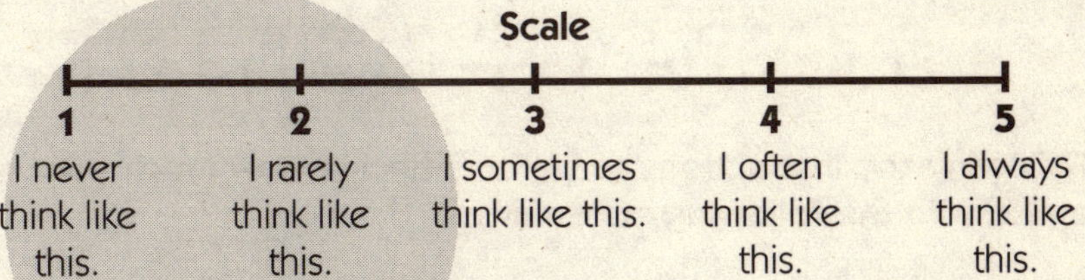

1. I wish I was like my best friend. She's really popular compared to me.

2. I can't wear this, it makes me look awful.

3. I hope the teacher doesn't pick me – I'll go bright red.

4. Look at that lot laughing. I bet they're laughing at me.

5. I could never stand up and make a speech. I'd just die.

6. I'm not good at anything.

7. I wish I was better-looking.

Now add up your scores. The total is your subscore 1.

STATE OF BEING

Following the instructions as before, decide how much you agree with the following statements.

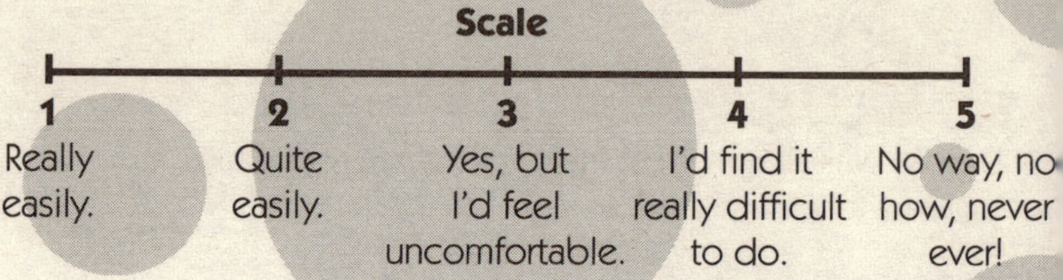

8. I could make an unprepared speech in front of 100 people.

9. I could organize a money-raising event for my favourite charity.

10. I could stick up for someone who was being bullied by a really popular girl.

11. I could represent my school in a national competition.

12. I could write a story that I think is good enough for submission to the school magazine.

13. I could audition for the school show and really believe I'll get the leading role.

14. I could start a petition about something I feel strongly about and persuade others to sign it.

15. I could do my Christmas tap-dancing and singing-duck routine for a dare in the middle of the local shopping centre.

Now add up your scores. The total is your subscore 2.

YOU ARE WHO YOU ARE

Once again, following the instructions as above, see how strongly you agree with these statements.

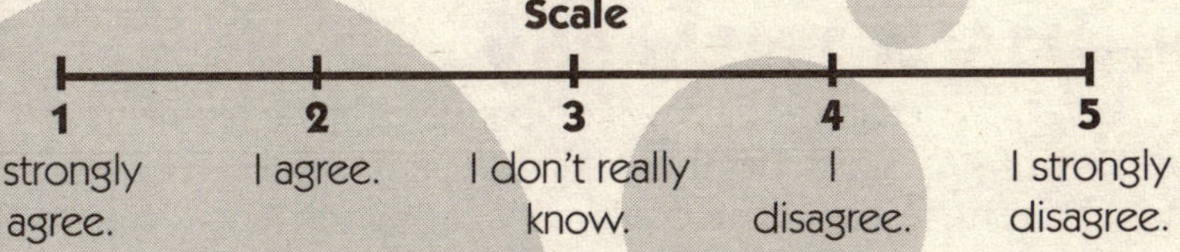

16. No matter what I can or can't do, I'm a very special person.

17. Being loud doesn't equal being confident.

18. Nothing scares me.

19. I love being me.

20. I'm really popular.

21. There's nothing I can't do if I set my mind to it.

22. I look great.

23. Everybody has something they can really succeed at.

Now add up your scores. The total is your subscore 3.

So how did you do? If you add your three subscores together, you will get your total confidence rating!

84–115 A Little Shy

Oh dear, we're feeling a bit down on ourselves at the moment, aren't we? Try to remember that just because you're a bit shy doesn't mean you can't have confidence in yourself. Some very shy people have some of the most public and demanding jobs possible, and they're very confident in what they do. Try to think of at least one thing about yourself that you really like, or one thing that you are really good at. And remember, just because someone's loud and in your face, it doesn't necessarily mean they're brimming with confidence either. In fact, often it's just the opposite. A big show of bravado can cover the fact that someone's actually scared stiff. Whenever you have a negative thought about yourself from now on, try to push it away with a positive thought.
Key word: anxious

51–83 More Than Enough

You're doing just fine. You get done what you want to get done, and if you ever have a moment of self-doubt you can talk yourself out of it ... usually. Sometimes your core of confidence melts away and you find yourself tongue-tied, stammering and red in the face,

but don't worry about it. It happens to everybody at one time or another – that's what being human's all about. And at least you have the honesty to admit that sometimes keeping a brave face on things is difficult to do. Anyway, it's not a daily occurrence, is it? You've certainly got more than enough confidence to carry you through.
Key word: balanced

23–50 Bags of It

Wowee! You really do feel good about yourself, don't you? That's great! You feel there's nothing you can't achieve in life if you really want to and you just love being you. But remember, other people don't always feel as confident as you do and you might have to be careful not to trample on others in your enthusiasm to get where you want to go. Sometimes it can be healthy to have a little moment of self-doubt, if only to help you reflect and make sure that what you're doing is definitely the right thing for you. You've got bags of confidence, so put it to good use and you could really go places!
Key word: super-confident

Tommy Girl

Are you a tomboy or a girly girl?
Take the test to find out.

Start Here
Can you give as good as you get with the loud-boy class joker?

Are you fearless: climbing trees, touching snakes ... easy?

Is your best buddy a boy?

Do you prefer a nice dress to trousers and trainers?

Are you quite happy making a fool of yourself in public?

Do you think girl and boy bands are a bit on the drippy side?

Were you the only person on the planet not interested in the World Cup?

Are you a practical joker?

Do you prefer to hang out with boys rather than girls?

In lessons, does the boys being stupid really wind you up?

Do you have nicknames for all your pals?

Do you find 'girls' sports like netball a bit on the soft side?

Do you think girls should look like girls?

Do you treat boys and girls exactly the same?

Is your bedroom a state?

Do you think ayone who burps is totally gross?

On holiday are you just as happy go-carting as sunbathing?

Does your mother go on at you all the time about your scruffy appearance?

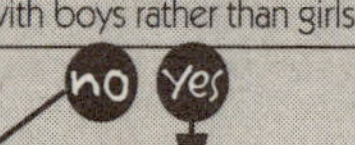

Lady Jane   Middle Ground   Tomboy

Middle Ground

You're a really well-balanced individual and, what's more, you seem to have a knack for getting on with everybody, male and female. You don't worry about how you should behave with boys or girls, you're just 'you' and they'll just have to take you as you are. Good for you!

Key word: **balanced**

Tomboy

Blimey, you're a bit of a tomboy, aren't you? No wonder your mum gives you grief. But don't worry. If you're happier kicking a ball than kicking back with some sparkly nail varnish, you do just that. You're lucky enough to live in a world where girls can have as many opportunities as boys, so go for it. But remember, there's nothing wrong with being female and you can have a good giggle with the girls too, you know.

Key word: **strong**

Lady Jane

You can't see anything appealing about being a boy. Boys are an alien species to you. You think they're loud, smelly, rough and, at times, downright scary. If you feel happy in a frock, you wear it, babe! But give the boys a chance. They're not all bad and are probably just as confused about you.

Key word: **feminine**

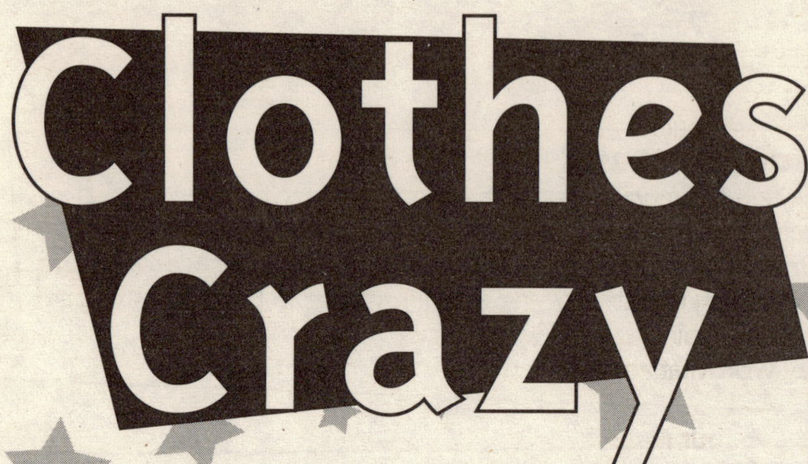

Are you a shopoholic with a passion for fashion, or do clothes leave you cold? Take the test to find out.

1. It's your birthday and your sister's said she'll buy you some perfume. Have you requested:

A. The latest designer scent? If she doesn't get it you'll just die!

B. Eco-friendly, not tested on animals, fresh, clean spray? You care about you but you care about the world too.

C. Something she likes? She's got much better taste than you.

D. That she decides? You couldn't care less: they all smell the same and she's only getting you perfume because she works at the chemist and gets a discount!

2. You're going out with your mates. Do you:

A. Have your perfect outfit laid out on the bed ready? You know just what to wear and have had it ready for over a week.
B. Have a quick scan in your wardrobe and pick out just the thing?
C. Think you know what you want to wear, put it on, take it off, put something else on, and repeat this procedure about 50,000 times before ending up back with outfit number one?
D. Wear what you've been wearing all day?

3. Do your mates:

A. Always turn to you for advice about clothes?
B. Sometimes ask you, but also advise you? It's a two-way street.
C. Rarely ask you? They can't get a word in, you're so busy asking them for advice.
D. Never talk to you about clothes – what would be the point?

4. Is shopping:

A. Your dream pastime? If money were no object you wouldn't do anything else – ever.
B. Good fun? You like to go shopping with your mates, try stuff on and have a laugh.
C. Fun, but a bit traumatic too? You're never sure you've bought the right thing and always end up taking some-thing back.
D. A form of long, drawn-out torture?

5. Do you see yourself as:
A. A trendsetter? You've always got whatever's 'in' before anyone else even knows about it. And when they realize it's 'in', as far as you're concerned it's already 'out'!
B. A fashionable dresser? You like to keep up with the latest styles but you're going to buy something because you look good in it rather than because it's the height of fashion.
C. A bit of a dull dresser? You'd like to wear more trendy stuff, but you're just not sure that you can carry it off.
D. A comfortable dresser? You like to be able to relax in your threads – you're not some kind of clothes horse.

6. Your mate's new outfit really doesn't suit her. Do you:
A. Tell her straight? Honesty's always the best policy, even if it hurts her feelings.
B. Tell her, but only if she asks? If she's not sure, you'll give her your opinion, but if she's happy with her look, that's fine by you.
C. Say nothing? It's probably really fashionable.
D. Not even notice? Who cares what she looks like?

7. Your friends are having a chat about clothes and fashion. Do you:
A. Feel bored? As if they know anything about clothes!
B. Join in? It's great flicking through the mags and checking out the latest looks.
C. Listen in quietly? Maybe you can pick up some top tips.
D. Feel bored? You really have nothing to say.

8. When you go shopping, do you:
A. Always buy something new and unconventional?
B. Go for something trendy that suits you?
C. Look at the really hip stuff longingly, then chicken out and go for the same old styles you wear all the time?
D. I told you, I don't do shopping!

9. It's Sunday morning and you're still in bed. Your mum wants you to nip down to the local shops to get a pint of milk. Do you:

A. Spend half an hour pondering over what to wear, and another half an hour getting ready, by which time your mum's given up and gone herself?

B. Pull on your jeans and top and go?

C. Pull on your jeans and top and go, but hope no one sees you as you're sure you're not looking very good?

D. Pull on whatever's nearest on the floor, even if it's your worst old tracksuit bottoms?

Mainly 'A's: Fashion Victim

Hey, girl, lighten up! You're a little obsessed with the way you look and you're becoming a bit of a bore. Fashion's fun, but you don't want to let it rule your life. You really shouldn't judge people by the way they look, you know. It's absolutely no indication of what they're like on the inside. Sure, it's nice to make the best of yourself, but get your priorities right. There's a lot more to life than making sure you've got the right label on your pants. Most people just aren't that hung up about what you look like, so try to calm down a bit on the clothing front. You'll probably find that you still look just as good, but you'll have a bit more fun doing it!

Key word: judgemental

Mainly 'B's: Friend to Fashion

Well, you seem pretty sorted! You like to look good and you're determined to make the best of yourself, but you're not going to let fashion rule your life. You've got a knack for combining clothing and coming out looking great, but you know it's not the most important thing in life and that clothes don't make the man (or the girl, for that matter!). Keep it up – you're way cool!

Key word: cool

Mainly 'C's: Clothing Crisis

Mmmm, you like clothes and in your mind's eye you're about as hip and happening as they come. But, in reality, you haven't quite got the confidence to carry it off and tend to go for the same sort of outfits again and again. Worry not, it's easier to give yourself a makeover than you might think. Just take it a step at a time: try a different top, or a change in footwear. Why not ask your friends if you can try on some of their clothes to give you a new idea of what might suit you? And remember, you can always play around with your hair if you want to give your look a bit of a boost. Good luck, and here's looking at the all-new you!

Key word: follower

Mainly 'D's: Couldn't Care Less

Well, well, well, you're one of those rare creatures who simply isn't that interested in clothes. You like yourself just fine the way you are and don't feel the need to mess with the packaging. But remember, every now and again, when you need to make a good impression, clothes can help you do just that, so don't ignore them altogether. But, for the time being, hang loose if you're happy with the way you are, and you'll find other people will be too!

Key word: unconventional

Food Fan or Fusspot?

Can you tell one end of a stick of celery from another, or would you not know a vindaloo from a vol-au-vent? Once you've sorted out your own kitchen know-how, why not try this quiz on a chum and see how she measures up on the food front?

1. What is ciabatta?
A. A type of Italian bread
B. A type of Chinese cabbage
C. A hot spice

2. You're invited to your friend's house for tea. Her mum is German and cooks a big stew with traditional dumplings and some red cabbage cooked in sugar, cloves and vinegar. You've never tried anything like it before. Are you:
A. So sure you're not going to like it that you change your mind about staying, make up an excuse and leave ASAP?
B. Really excited? It's better than having the same old stuff you alway have at home.
C. Not sure you'll like it, but you're prepared to give it a try anyway? You never know, it might be the best thing you've ever tasted!

3. What is chow mein?

A. A Chinese dish made with noodles
B. A Greek dish made with rice
C. A Finnish dish made with fish

4. You're on a school trip and everyone's swapping sandwiches on the bus. Do you:

A. Get in there quick – some people seem to have some really tasty treats in their packed lunches?
B. Decide not to get involved – you're perfectly happy with your usual selection, thank you very much?
C. Swap a couple of bits but hold on to the rest – after all, if you don't like your swaps, you might starve?

5. What is paella?

A. A Spanish dish made with rice
B. A Turkish pie
C. A dessert made with pears

6. If you had to list all the dishes/ingredients that you don't like, would your list be:

A. Quite long – with at least fifteen things on it?
B. Medium length – with about five major dislikes?
C. Pretty short – there are only one or two things you really can't stand?

7. If you had to make some food for a vegetarian, would you:
A. Have no idea what to do, so just give them meat and two veg without the meat?
B. Have no idea but enjoy the challenge of finding something new – you're sure there must be loads of things to make, but you'd have to have a quick flip through a recipe book?
C. Have no problems, because you're a vegetarian yourself?

8. What is chicken vindaloo?
A. A Swedish chicken stew
B. A hot and spicy Asian curry dish
C. A French dish made with wine

9. If you go to a restaurant, do you:
A. Always ask for something that's familiar to you, then you know you'll like it?
B. Ask for something a bit different and then worry that you won't like it?
C. Ask for something unusual that you've never had before? You're sure it'll be great, but if you don't like it it's not a problem, you'll just know for next time.

10. Where do Seville oranges come from?
A. France
B. Spain
C. Serbia

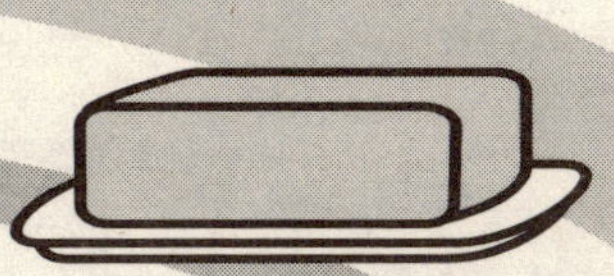

A. Leave that bit of the meal to one side of your plate and apologize, explaining that it's something you don't like? You wouldn't want them to give it to you ever again, would you?

B. Struggle to eat it – it would be rude not to – but maybe leave a little bit at the end, saying you're just too full to manage it?

C. It just wouldn't happen – there's virtually nothing you don't like!

12. Your friend's busy tucking into something that looks pretty disgusting. Do you:

A. Say, 'That looks horrible … can I have a try?'

B. Wrinkle your nose and say, 'Yuck, I just don't know how you can eat that'?

C. Say nothing? You're afraid she might offer you some and that you'd feel obliged to give it a go!

13. Do you:

A. Love cooking – you enjoy trying out new recipes?

B. Hate cooking – it's boring and you're no good at it anyway?

C. Quite like cooking but tend not to go for anything too adventurous?

14. If you went abroad, would you:
A. Be dead excited about trying out the local dishes?
B. Try something a bit different but that reminds you of what you eat at home?
C. Starve? There's nothing you recognize, and if you don't know exactly what it is there's no way you're eating it!

Now add up your scores:

1.	A.10	B.0	C.0	2.	A.0	B.10	C.5
3.	A.10	B.0	C.0	4.	A.10	B.0	C.5
5.	A.10	B.0	C.0	6.	A.0	B.5	C.10
7.	A.0	B.5	C.10	8.	A.0	B.10	C.0
9.	A.0	B.5	C.10	10.	A.0	B.10	C.0
11.	A.0	B.5	C.10	12.	A.10	B.0	C.5
13.	A.10	B.0	C.5	14.	A.10	B.5	C.0

100—140 Food Fan

You love trying new food. There just might be a taste sensation waiting around the corner that you haven't experienced yet and you'd hate to miss out. Every day's an education for your taste buds and the more adventurous the dish, the more you fancy giving it a go. You love getting in the kitchen, pulling on your pinny and rifling through the recipe books for something new to create. I see a career as a top chef looming.

Key word: adventurous

40—99 Faint-hearted Foodie

You like the idea of new and exciting dishes, but you're rather a wimp when it comes to actually taking the plunge and trying something a bit different. Still, if you carry on the way you're going, you'll soon have quite a range of dishes under your belt (literally!) and you'll be able to recognize what you do and don't like. Good for you for giving it a go!

Key word: tryer

0—39 Cuisine Cautious

You really like to play it safe when it comes to mealtimes. There are a few things you know you like and you're sticking to them. You don't want to try anything new, as you're pretty sure you won't like it. The trouble is, unless you try, you'll never really know, and you could be missing out on a whole galaxy of delicious taste experiences. Still, all the more for the rest of us, I suppose!

Key word: conservative

JUST THE JOB

If you had a crystal ball, wouldn't it be fab to have a look and see what you'll be up to in, say, ten or fifteen years' time? Well, you can forget all that crystal-gazing stuff. Just try out this cracking careers quiz and find out where you might be heading.

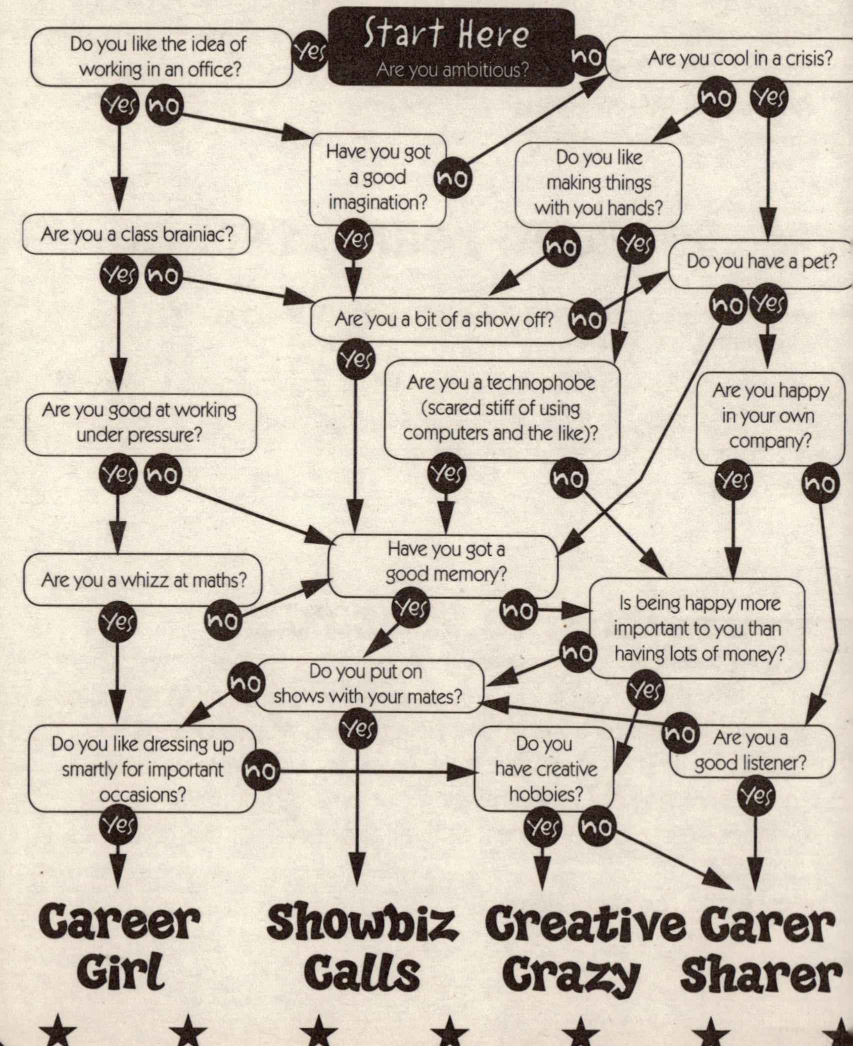

Showbiz Calls

You love being the centre of attention – telling jokes and always giving your mates a good laugh. You love being in the limelight and consider yourself pretty multi-talented when it comes to entertaining. So build on your strengths, work on your weaknesses and there's no reason why we shouldn't be seeing your name in lights some day real soon! Your ideal job would be: actress, TV presenter, dancer or holiday-camp rep.
Key word: performer

Career Girl

You're bright, hard-working and very keen to get ahead. You love a challenge, thrive under pressure and at times have a job keeping your competitive streak under control! You're full of energy and actually enjoy solving problems. So put your energies to good use and you could be a real high-flyer! Your ideal job would be: lawyer, stockbroker or journalist.
Key word: ambitious

Carer Sharer

You're calm, level-headed and a brilliant pal to have around in a crisis. You have more patience than most and really enjoy helping other people out. You're good as part of a team but can happily deal with people one to one. Money won't be as important to you as job satisfaction and you want to do something that makes a difference because … you're really ever so nice! Your ideal job would be: social worker, nurse, vet or teacher.
Key word: caring

Creative Crazy

You're a very creative type, always having a go at something new. You're happy beavering away on your own and love the fact that you can make something out of nothing. You're not looking for glamour or pots of money – art goes deeper than that. But one day you could find yourself famous for your paintings or sculptures! Your ideal job would be: artist, designer or gallery curator.
Key word: arty

Like all good citizens, you want to save the planet … or do you? Find out how much you really know about things eco-friendly. Are you an eco-warrior or an enviro-flop?

1. Do you think ozone is:
A. Something you get in aerosol cans?
B. A layer of protective gas surrounding our planet?
C. A new girl band?

2. Is global warming:
A. The overall rising of the temperature of the Earth?
B. The thing that makes some countries hotter than others?
C. A new boy band?

3. Do you know where your nearest recycling centre is?
A. Yes.
B. No.
C. What's a recycling centre?

4. When you brush your teeth, do you:
A. Leave the tap running the whole time?
B. Only have the tap on when you actually need it?
C. I never brush my teeth!

Queen

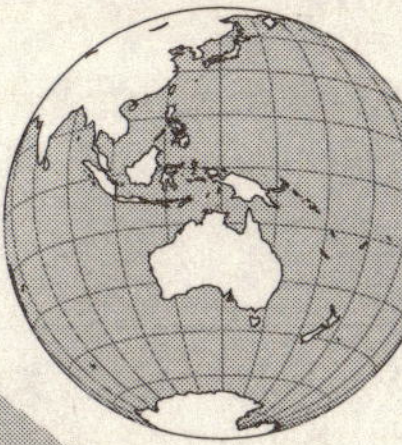

5. If you have to go over to your friend's house, which is five minutes away by car, do you:

A. Get someone to give you a lift?

B. Walk or ride your bike – it only takes a little longer and it's much better for you?

C. Make them come to you – you can't be bothered to leave the house?

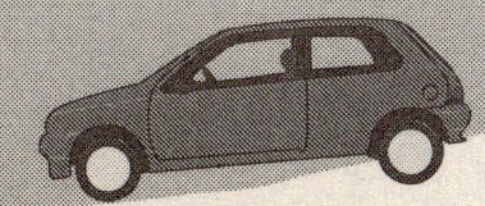

6. You're in your bedroom and you get called downstairs for tea. Do you:

A. Make sure you've switched the light off before you leave the room?

B. Rush downstairs, remember halfway and rush back up to switch the light off?

C. Leave the light on, then you won't have to bother when you come back up?

7. Your family don't separate any rubbish for recycling and you know it would be better if they did. Do you:

A. Suggest they start and offer to label boxes for bottles and papers and find out about the nearest recycling centre?

B. Make a vague suggestion but don't really pursue it, just taking the odd bottle to the bottle bank every now and again?

C. Do nothing about it?

8. When you get a new notebook, do you:

A. Make sure you fill each page so that every bit of paper is covered before you get a new one?

B. Write a couple of lines on each page before starting a new one – it's so nice having a clean white page to write on?

C. Write on every other page?

9. When you buy a birthday card or a Christmas card, do you look for:
A. Something you like? If it's made from recycled paper or the profits go to a charity, that's a bonus.
B. Only something that's made from recycled paper and helps a charitable organization?
C. Never buy cards!

10. You've read that putting a lemonade bottle full of water in your toilet cistern will help you use less water when you flush. Do you:
A. Put one in the cistern without telling your family and wait to see if anyone notices the difference?
B. Suggest to your family that that's what you might do, but never actually get round to it?
C. Do nothing? There's no way you're having anything to do with the toilet!

11. You read in the newspaper that a local company is dumping loads of nasty chemicals into the canal near your home.
Do you:

A. Start a campaign to stop them, including meetings at the town hall, a 1,000-name petition and a head-to-head confrontation with the company concerned?

B. Write a letter to the company asking them to stop, but let it go at that when you don't hear anything back?

C. Do nothing? It's not as if you can single-handedly change the world, is it? So why bother?

Now add up your scores:

1. A.10 B.15 C.5	2. A.15 B.10 C.5	3. A.15 B.10 C.5
4. A.10 B.15 C.5	5. A.10 B.15 C.5	6. A.15 B.10 C.5
7. A.15 B.10 C.5	8. A.15 B.10 C.5	9. A.10 B.15 C.5
10. A.15 B.10 C.5	11. A.15 B.10 C.5	

126–165 Eco-warrior

Wow! You really are keen to save the planet. You're prepared to take action and get things done, even if it means a little more effort on your part. You're doing brilliantly and all the small steps you take will help to influence the overall picture. You really care about the environment and are switched-on enough to know that it's up to us to protect our planet for future generations.

Key word: eco-friendly

76–125 Eco-wimp

Well, your heart's in the right place, but you seem to lack the courage of your convictions. You have an idea about what needs doing, it's just that you can't really muster the energy to do it. You don't want to have to stand up for what you believe in because it's too much hassle. But if you really put your mind to it and got a little bit more organized, you'd be surprised how easy it is to be really eco-friendly with hardly any effort at all. Go on! Give it a whirl, girl!

Key word: lazybones

55–75 Eco-what?

Uh-oh! You're not exactly the best-informed person in the world when it comes to environmental issues. Maybe it's time you started giving the state of the planet a bit of thought. Do you really think it's OK to rely on others to keep the planet safe for you? You've got plenty of room for improvement, so the only way is up! If you live on it, you're responsible for it. You don't need to make life difficult for yourself. Simple things like switching lights off and shutting doors to keep the heat in save energy and resources without any hardship to you. So shape up and start doing your bit for planet Earth.

Key word: irresponsible

Face ★ It!

Your eyes are the windows to your soul, so the saying goes. But can the rest of your gorgeous features tell you anything about your personality? Do a fun photofit of yourself and see if anything from your eyebrows to your nose can provide an insight into the true you! Your key words are in bold throughout.

Eye Colour

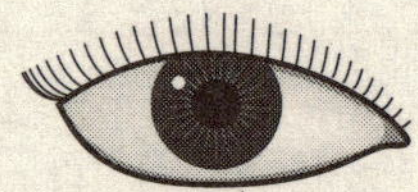

Blue or brown

You are a very trustworthy type. **Honest** and reliable, you try hard never to let anyone down. But you're also quite an easygoing sort, so you don't get too hung up about things if they're not going your way. You simply shrug and say, 'Ho-hum, c'est la vie!' – and why not?

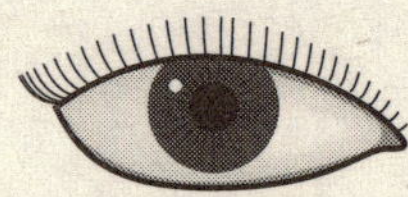

Grey

You are generally a pretty happy person, but you can get a bit bad-tempered if you don't get your own way. **Moody** grey eyes often mean moody by nature. It's not a problem, though, as you actually quite like having a bit of a ding-dong!

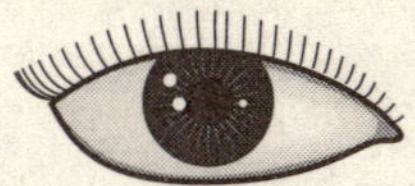

Green or black

You could be the sort of person who likes to keep all their cards up their sleeves. You don't give away much about yourself and can even come across as **mysterious**. But some people find you intriguing and would love to be your friend, so they can find out just what really is going on behind those secretive peepers!

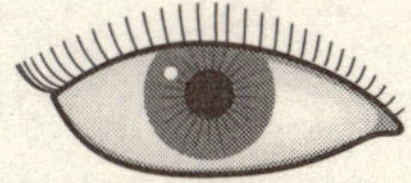

Hazel

You are quite a **popular** type. You thrive on company and love being the centre of attention. You may even consider yourself among the top ten of class jokers, with a hilarious jape at the ready for every occasion!

Eye Shape

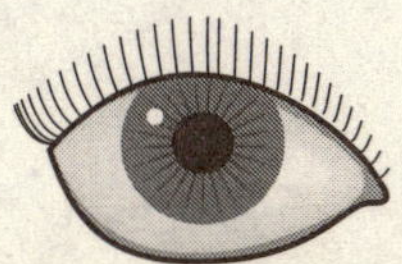

Large and round

You are usually warm-hearted and **giving**, but you're also quite wise and don't suffer fools gladly. Once you get to know someone and trust them, you're a true pal and a really great mate to have around.

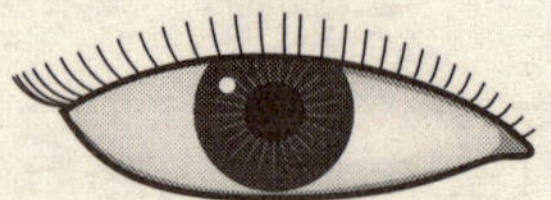

Almond

You're quite a **generous** type, with a really gentle side to your nature. You can be a bit of a softie and are quite easily moved to tears. You're caring and sharing and altogether rather lovely – ahhh!

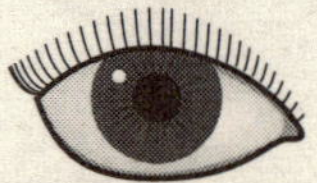

Small

You can be a little on the **shy** side and don't like to give too much away until you know someone really well. This means you can sometimes come across as a bit of a mystery girl, but that's no bad thing, as people often want to find out more about you, and when they do they realize just how nice you are!

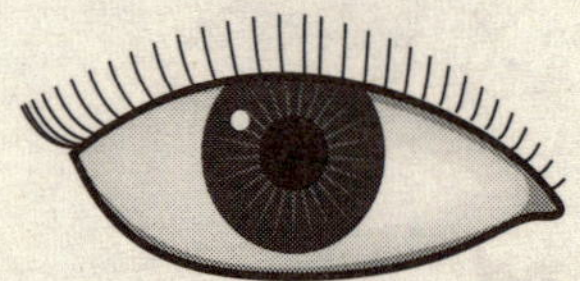

Big

You can sometimes come across as a bit of an **innocent** and, it must be said, you can be quite easily taken in by things. Watch out for your mates trying out their tricks on you, as they know you'll fall for it every time! But, hey, you don't really mind … You like being you, and sweet and innocent are lovely things to be!

Eyebrows

Half-moon

You can be a bit of a brainiac and quite highly strung. It's tough being the only **genius** in the family, but I guess you'll just have to learn to live with it – Einstein!

Arched

You're potential prime-minister material! You've got **leader** just stamped all over you. When you talk, others listen.

Bushy

You're loyal and **dependable** and a great person to have as a best friend. You try very hard not to let your friends down, you're trustworthy and would never tell a secret.

Thin and delicate

You are generally cool, **calm** and in control. It takes a lot to rattle you and you know how to keep your head in a crisis. You're a real organizer and can get your room shipshape in about thirty seconds flat!

Mouth

Small and pouting

You may need coaxing out of your shell a bit, as you can come over a little **shy**, but once you've relaxed in someone's company you're a real laugh to have around.

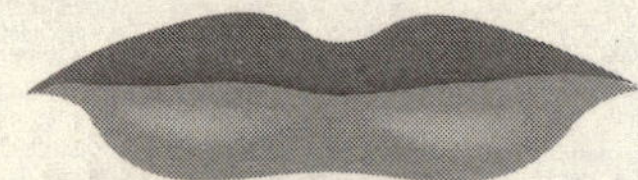

Downturned

You tend to be a bit of a **worrier** and can get wound up if your homework's late or you've misplaced your sports kit. But as soon as you've done the work or found the kit, you're able to relax again – until the next crisis arises!

Large and upturned

Hi there, little Ms **Extrovert**! You're loud and you're proud and you love playing to a crowd!

Thin

You're quite an **ambitious** type. You know what you want and you're prepared to work for it. You could be a real achiever!

The Nose Knows

Straight

A **trustworthy** type. Anyone could tell you their most dreadful secret, safe in the knowledge that you'd keep it – for ever if necessary. What a rock!

Turns up

What a **sweetie**! You care about your friends and you're probably a real sucker for little fluffy animals too!

Turns down

You're very focused and **hard-working**. You want to do well in life and you're prepared to put in the groundwork.

Broad

You're a real friend to those in need, a great **listener** and good at giving advice. Your friends tend to treat you as a resident agony aunt!

Ear-ear

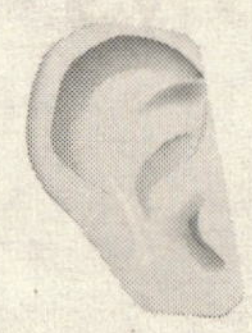

Rectangular
A very **loyal** character. You'll stand by someone to the bitter end.

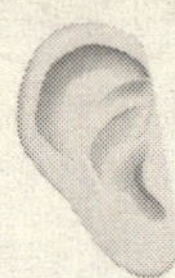

Small
You may be a little on the **shy** side and can take a while to get to know people, but once you do you're warm and friendly and a pleasure to have around.

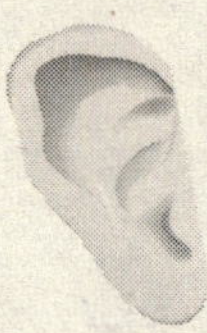

Wide top
You're a very **honest** person. You don't like dishonesty and will try to avoid anyone you think is not quite as straightforward as you tend to be.

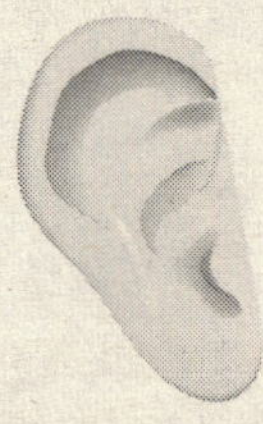

Big
You're kind, **generous** and giving. What a star!

Friends For Ever

Best Mate Test

So you think you know each other inside out? Find out if you really do in this friendship test!

Get together with your best buddy and, without conferring, answer the following questions about each other. Note down your answers on a piece of paper. Remember, no talking to each other – this is a test!

You on you

Your worst habit is?

The word/phrase
you use most often is?

Your fave part of
your body is?

Which of these words
describes you best:
kind / confident / funny?

How tall are you?

What's your fave
flavour milkshake?

What's your fave band?

What size shoes do you wear?

What's your fave sport?

Are you most at home
in a cute little dress, jeans
or smart trousers?

You on your best mate

Her worst habit is?

The word/phrase she uses
most often is?

Her fave part of her body is?

Which of these words
describes her best:
kind / confident / funny?

How tall is she?

What's her fave
flavour milkshake?

What's her fave band?

What size shoes does she wear?

What's her fave sport?

Is she most at home
in a cute little dress, jeans
or smart trousers?

Now compare your answers. How many things did you get right about each other and what does that say about just how well you really do know each other? Score a point for each correct answer.

7–10 Bosom Buddies

Wow! Do you two ever spend any time apart or are you joined at the hip? You've got a very close friendship. You know each other really well and you tell each other everything. If you ever needed a shoulder to cry on, you'd know just where to turn. Don't let anyone come between you guys, you've got something really special going there.

Key word: soulmate

3–6 Mutual Mates

You've got a good easygoing relationship. You're very special to each other, but you don't feel the need to live in each other's pockets. You're happy to hang out alone or in a crowd and you're in tune with each other's loves and hates without invading any space. Way to go!

Key word: independent

0–3 Pathetic Pals

Oh dear, there seems to be a breakdown in communication here somewhere. You're not exactly in tune with what goes on in your friend's head. But hey, opposites often attract, so it isn't necessarily the end of the world. But if you want your friendship to last, you might try getting to know each other a little bit better!

Key word: incommunicado

★ FRIENDSHIP ★ CONSEQUENCES

Sometimes you and your best mate do the most crazy things. To find out just how mad your madcap antics might get, read on!

Find a dice and take turns to throw it. Read the snippet below that corresponds with the number thrown. Carry on throwing the dice and work your way through every section to see just what a nutty couple you are. If you don't have a dice, just take turns choosing a number from 1 to 6 – but no peeking at the answers!

So, you and your best mate are having a day out ... Play on to see how it'll affect the rest of your lives!

1. You meet:
1: at your house
2: on top of the Empire State Building
3: at the swimming baths
4: at the shopping centre
5: on an alien spaceship
6: in a top-secret location

2. You're wearing:
1: your new designer suit
2: a bikini and a flowery swimming hat
3: dungarees and a pair of wellie boots
4: jeans, a T and trainers
5: nothing!
6: a caftan

3. She's wearing:
1: a balaclava and ski suit
2: a wet suit, flippers and a snorkel
3: a bin bag
4: jeans, a T and trainers
5: overalls and boots
6: a smile!

4. You go:
1: to the cinema
2: ballistic!
3: shopping
4: in at the deep end
5: for a pizza
6: to another planet

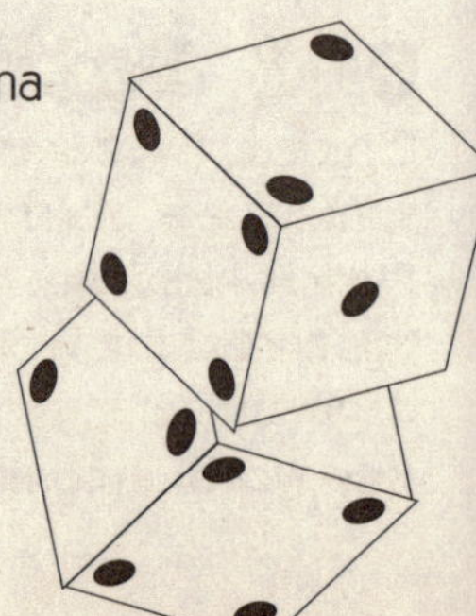

5. She says to you:
1: 'What do you think of my outfit?'
2: 'I've done more lengths than you.'
3: 'Good movie.'
4: 'What's your problem?'
5: 'Mmmm yum scrum.'
6: 'Take me to your leader.'

6. You say to her:
1: 'I think I'm drowning.'
2: 'Not bad, bit long though.'
3: 'Mine! What's yours?'
4: 'Mmmm, ish delish.'
5: 'Beam me up, Mummy.'
6: 'Eee, you look gorgeous.'

7. Your nickname for her is:
1: Windbag
2: Stinko
3: Gorgeo
4: Raymond
5: Noodle nog
6: Grouch

8. She gives you:
1: a headache
2: an alien virus
3: a diving lesson
4: her burnt crust
5: some popcorn off the floor
6: a few fashion tips

9. You decide to:
1: go for an early shower
2: seek medical attention
3: head for home
4: get a doggy bag
5: give her a serious makeover
6: make like a banana – and split!

10. The consequence is:
1: you'll be friends for ever
2: it's all over between you
3: you know she's nuts
4: you have a new and deeper understanding
5: things'll never be the same
6: nothing's changed

Wow! Are you two crazy ladies or what?

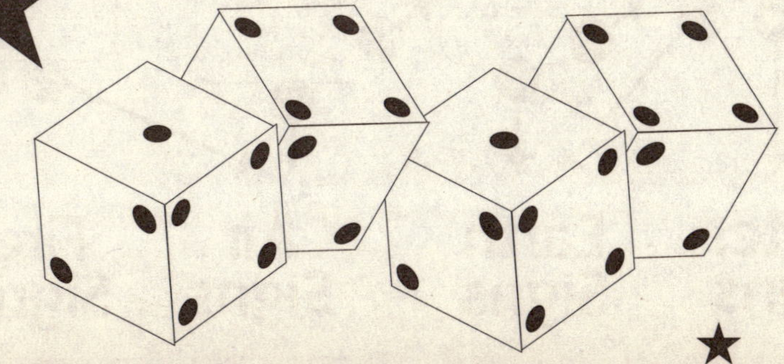

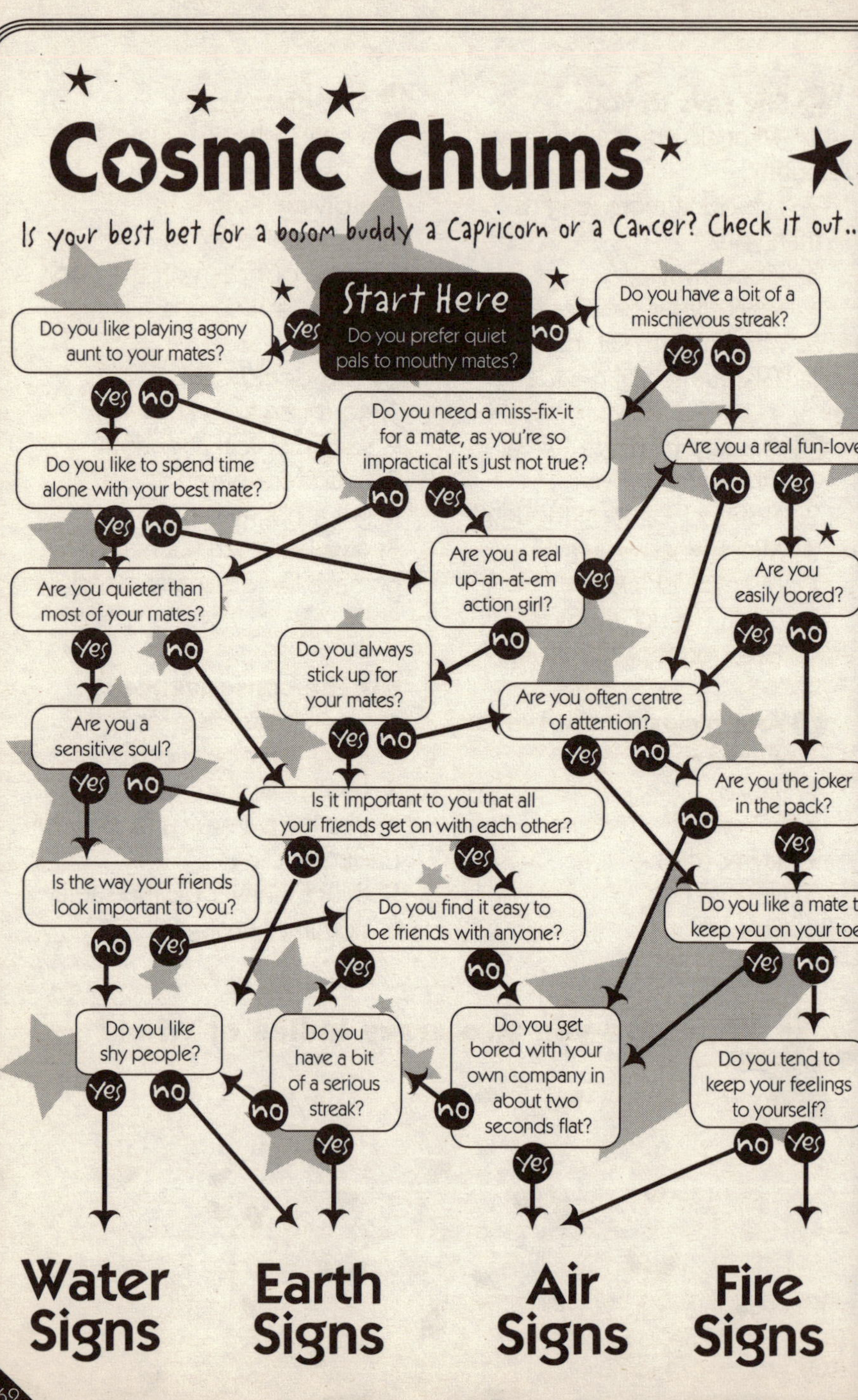

Cosmic Chums
Is your best bet for a bosom buddy a Capricorn or a Cancer? Check it out...
Start Here
Do you prefer quiet pals to mouthy mates?
Yes
no
Do you like playing agony aunt to your mates?
Do you have a bit of a mischievous streak?
Yes
no
Yes
no
Do you like to spend time alone with your best mate?
Do you need a miss-fix-it for a mate, as you're so impractical it's just not true?
Are you a real fun-love
no
Yes
Yes
no
no
Yes
Are you quieter than most of your mates?
Are you a real up-an-at-em action girl?
Are you easily bored?
Yes
no
Yes
Yes
no
Are you a sensitive soul?
Do you always stick up for your mates?
Are you often centre of attention?
Yes
no
Yes
no
Yes
no
Is the way your friends look important to you?
Is it important to you that all your friends get on with each other?
Are you the joker in the pack?
no
no
Yes
Yes
no
Yes
Do you like shy people?
Do you have a bit of a serious streak?
Do you find it easy to be friends with anyone?
Do you get bored with your own company in about two seconds flat?
Do you like a mate t keep you on your toe
Do you tend to keep your feelings to yourself?
Yes
no
no
Yes
no
Yes
Yes
no
no
Yes
Yes
no
Water Signs
Earth Signs
Air Signs
Fire Signs

Water Signs

The mates for you are water signs: **Cancer, Scorpio and Pisces**
Choosing water signs means that you're probably quite a quiet person yourself. The water girls tend to be sensitive and dreamy and at times a bit on the intense side. If you've got a water-sign buddy, you'll probably like to spend a lot of time with each other and develop quite a deep friendship. But watch out, cross a water sign and they can flare up and go all fiery – yikes!
Key word: dreamy

Earth Signs

The mates for you are earth signs: **Taurus, Virgo and Capricorn**
Earth-sign people make great mates! Not only are they very practical and hard-working, but they're also incredibly loyal. They'll be prepared to stand by you through thick and thin and will happily lend a hand whenever you need them. Basically if you team up with an earth sign, you've got a friend for life!
Key word: supported

Air Signs

The mates for you are air signs: **Gemini, Libra and Aquarius**
Air signs are usually quite popular people. They're fun to be with and pretty unpredictable. If you pick an air sign for a chum you're in for a roller-coaster ride of fun, with absolutely never a dull moment. So hang on tight, it's going to be an exhilarating ride!
Key word: exciting

Fire Signs

The mates for you are fire signs: **Aries, Leo and Sagittarius**
If you want a friend to light up your life, go for an energetic, enthusiastic fire sign. They love having a laugh, are happy-go-lucky and really do just want to have fun. They can be a little self-centred, but they don't mean to be … they just don't always understand that not everyone thinks every idea they ever had is the best idea ever. And don't forget, fire signs have feelings too, but they're not very good at showing them. So to be their best mate you have to be a bit of a mind-reader too!
Key word: fun-loving

soul sisters

You think you and your best mate know each other so well you can read each other's minds. Try this test to see if the same things make you tick or if really you're walking to a different beat …

Take it in turns with your best friend to go through the following two-part questionnaire. Write your answers on a piece of paper and don't tell each other what you've put down. Once you've both finished, compare your answers using the score guide at the bottom of each section.

Section One

Answer the following questions twice: once for yourself and once how you think your friend would answer.

1. You get the lead part in a film. Is it:

A. A daredevil action film in which you hack your way through a jungle and swing across ravines without a moment's hesitation?
B. A romantic comedy with you as the leading lady, and you look lovely?
C. A costume drama – you just love all those old-fashioned outfits?

2. You like to read books that are:

A. Funny – you like a laugh.
B. Sad – there's nothing like a weepy.
C. Factual – you like to find new things out.

3. Look at the following three pictures. Which one appeals to you most?

4. If you were a car you'd be:

A. A mini – little and cute and funky.
B. A jeep – rugged and adventurous.
C. A Porsche – glamorous and fast.

5. You've just landed on a desert island. Is it:
A. Barren and rocky and desolate?
B. Lush and green, with dense foliage and screeching parrots?
C. Hot and sandy, with the odd shady palm tree?

Section One scores: score 10 points if your own answer matched the answer your friend picked for herself; your friend scores 10 points each time the answer she put for you matches what you put for yourself.

Section Two
Read the following statements. Both note down the ones you think are true about your friendship.

1. I can tell when she's upset without her saying anything.
2. We never argue.
3. I often know what she's going to say before she says it.
4. We like the same music.
5. If I'm thinking about her she'll quite often ring or come round unexpectedly.
6. We always tell the truth to each other and don't have any secrets.
7. When we go shopping we always pick the same clothes.
8. She can make me laugh even when I feel sad.
9. I'd trust her with any secret.
10. If we went out to eat, we'd both choose the same food.
11. She usually appears in my dreams.

Section Two scores: score 10 points each for every statement you both picked; subtract 5 points if you or your mate picked a statement and the other one of you didn't.

Now add your scores from Sections One and Two together for your total sister score!

110–160 Great Mates

Wow! Do you two know each other like the backs of your hands or what? It's as if you were separated at birth. You know exactly what's going on in your buddy's brain and, more often than not, you feel exactly the same way too! You truly are great mates, to the extent that sometimes you find it hard to remember that you can have fun with other people too. Yours is a really special friendship, built on total trust and understanding. What a lucky pair you are!

Key word: linked

60–109 Best of Buddies

Ahh … nice. You're firm friends and you don't care who knows it. You're switched on to your buddy's thought waves without being a clone of her. You're able to have a great friendship without living in each other's pockets. You're happy to be independent too, and know when to give each other a bit of space. You share a lot of the same tastes but don't feel put off if your mate likes to do some things her own way. You're a coolsome twosome and that's just great!

Key word: comfortable

0–59 Dumb Chums!

You may well get on really fabulously, but you're not exactly switched on as to what makes each other tick. You really don't know if your mate's a fan of action-packed adventures or a sucker for anything soppy! But still, I guess it makes your relationship kind of interesting as you literally have no idea what your mate might say next. They say opposites attract and this may well be the case with you two … And let's face it, having done this questionnaire, you'll at least know more about each other than you did half an hour ago!

Key word: independent-minded

Are You Your Best Mate's Best Mate?

See how you rate as a best mate in this perceptive personality quiz. Be honest now, and have a particular friend in mind!

1. Your best friend wins the school poetry prize for her poem 'My Dog'. Are you:

A. Pleased for her – the prize is book tokens and you reckon she may buy you something? After all, you did help her find a rhyme for 'woofy'!

B. Pleased for her – she deserved to win?

C. Pleased, but a bit upset too? After all, that poem was really half your work as well … She always grabs the glory for things you've done together!

2. Your mate is having a birthday party. Do you:

A. Offer to help her organize it? That way you can get the best food and make sure the only games to be played are the ones you like.

B. Know all about it of course – it's a surprise party and you're the one organizing it!

C. Offer to help and then find yourself doing everything while your mate swans around having fun? But it is her birthday, so you try not to feel too bad about it.

3. Your friend's hamster, Bob, has just died. Do you:

A. Give her lots of sympathy, but secretly hope she gets over it quite quickly? She's not much fun when she's upset.

B. Provide a shoulder to cry on? You loved old Bob too.

C. Run around after her for weeks while she 'recovers'? It seems grief has made her incapable of doing even the simplest thing.

4. Your friend gets a new pet, Benny the puppy. She's besotted with him, spends all her time with him and talks about him constantly. Are you:

A. A bit jealous? She seems more interested in Benny than she is in you.

B. Glad for her? It's good to see her getting over the loss of Bob and Benny's really good fun too – you're her number-one dog-walking companion.

C. Pleased for her? After all, she lets you play with him and take him for walks too.

5. Your friend phones and invites you over to her house, but when you get there she says she's changed her mind and she's going out for the afternoon with her sister. Are you:

A. Not that bothered? There are plenty of other people you'd be just as happy to spend the afternoon with.

B. Seriously annoyed? She's being rude and inconsiderate and you would never think of treating her in such a way.

C. A bit hurt but OK? You can spend the afternoon with her another time.

6. You want to borrow a skirt you like from your friend to go skating in. Do you:

A. Go on and on and on about it until she gives in – pleading, begging and resorting to blackmail if you have to? Even if she doesn't really want to lend it to you, you have just got to have that skirt!

B. Ask her outright once and accept her yes or no?

C. Drop subtle hints like, 'I bet that red skirt is really comfy for skating in. I'd love a skirt like that,' and hope she cottons on and offers to lend it to you?

7. You've got quite a small bedroom with a single bed. When your friend stays over, do you:

A. Let her sleep on the floor?

B. Both sleep on the floor or top-to-toe in your bed – it's much more fun?

C. Give up your bed for her and sleep on the floor?

8. You lent your friend £1 about a week ago. She hasn't paid you back and you suspect she's forgotten about it. Do you:

A. Demand it back and have a bit of a go at her for putting you in the position where you had to ask for it?

B. Just say, 'By the way, you haven't forgotten that quid you owe me, have you?' It's no big deal!

C. Decide not to mention it – ever – and lend her another £1 next time she asks? After all, it's hardly her fault if she genuinely forgot about it.

9. When it's your birthday, do you expect your friend to:

A. Make a really big deal of it? After all, it only happens once a year!

B. Share in the whole day with you – that's what friends are for?

C. Get you a card and maybe a small gift? She doesn't need to bother with anything major if she doesn't want to.

10. Your best friend has had an argument with one of your other friends and tells you she doesn't think you should speak to this girl any more. Do you:

A. Ignore her? You know she doesn't seriously think she can tell you what to do. She's just a bit wound up at the moment.

B. Explain to your mate that it's not something you can really do – the quarrel's between the two of them and not you – but possibly avoid the girl in question for a couple of days until things have cooled off a bit?

C. Go along with her? If your best friend doesn't like the girl, then you don't like her either.

Mainly 'A's: Dominator

Oh dear, you can be a bit of a bossy-boots, can't you? And you can even go a bit green when your mate does well. True, it's nice to be top dog, but it's also nice to be able to feel good when someone else does well. Go easy on your friend and you might find you see your relationship in a whole new light. Give her a chance to shine and between the two of you you could make a pretty incredible team.

Key word: bossy

Mainly 'B's: Perfect Pal

Boy, oh boy, do you and your mate have things sorted! You care about your pal and are only too happy to put yourself out for her – probably because that's just what you'd expect in return. You know you can speak openly to your mate without upsetting the apple-cart and that she can do the same back to you. You understand that in relationships you need to allow for a little bit of give and take, and that's just fine by both of you. Seems like you were made for each other … ahhh!

Key word: balanced

Mainly 'C's: Power Potential

Yep, you need to increase your power factor a bit in this relation-ship. Do the words door and mat mean anything to you? No, really, it's not that bad – it's just that you have a tendency to let your pal lead while you follow on behind. That's OK to an extent – after all, some people are natural-born leaders – but if you feel strongly about something, don't you hesitate to stand up and speak your mind. If your friend's a true friend, she won't mind hearing what you have to say. In fact, you could find she rather likes it. So go on, girl, grab yourself a bit of power and balance this friendship out.

Key word: follower

What's She Like?

How well do you really know your friends? Why not find a quiet moment and do this quiz? Have a particular pal in mind and see if she's Debbie Dependable or Lucy Loud! And remember, this is one occasion where you might be best off keeping the results to yourself!

1. You get back your marks for a class test and, you can't believe it, you've come top. Is your mate:

A. Over the moon on your behalf – she even buys you a doughnut on the way home to celebrate?

B. Outwardly pleased for you, but you can tell that really she's a little put out by your success?

C. Not really interested? It's only a boring test after all.

D. Well impressed, and she lets everybody in town know about it by shouting your name, followed by the word 'brainiac', all the way home?

2. Your friend is invited to a birthday party at her cousin's house. Her house is really posh and your friend knows you've been dying to see it for ages. Does she:

A. Invite you along with about another ten other friends – the more the merrier has always been her philosophy?

B. Invite only people she thinks are 'cool' – you just have to hope that includes you?

C. Invite you, but only so she can keep going on about what a big favour she's done you and how fantastic her cousin is?

D. Invite you, of course – she's your mate, isn't she?

3. You and your mates have all tried out for a part in the school show. You get a part but your mate doesn't. Is she:

A. Really annoyed? She knows she's better than all the other people (including you) who got picked, it was just the drama teacher couldn't take the competition, that's all!

B. Disappointed, but glad for you? She even offers to help you learn your lines!

C. Gutted? It would have been such a laugh – she was really looking forward to all the messing around backstage!

D. Not bothered – who wants to be in a stupid little school show anyway?

4. You're on your way to swimming when you call in at your mate's house and realize you've forgotten your costume. Does she:

A. Lend you a really horrible old one of hers, saying her nicer costume is in the wash, then look smug the whole time you're at the pool as she glides past in her trendy little number?

B. Lend you her brand-new costume and wear her old one instead?

C. Get her two holiday bikinis out and swap the tops and bottoms so you can wear half each – she seems to think that's really funny?

D. Lend you an old costume of hers, but only if you promise not to talk to her while you're at the pool, in case anyone sees and thinks she's actually friends with someone who'd wear that old thing?

5. You're about to go out with your friend when your mum says you have to take the dog for a walk first. Does your friend:

A. Offer to come with you and keep you company?

B. Offer to come with you, but rush off to get her pedigree pooch first?

C. Offer to come with you, and spend the whole walk pretending to be a dog?

D. Wait for you in the house – dog-walking's just not where she's at?

6. Your auntie's a famous TV actress and she's coming to stay for a week. Does your friend:

A. Tell you all about *her* auntie, who's actually much more famous than yours?

B. Act normal – she's your friend after all, not your auntie's?

C. Come round and ask your auntie about 50,000 questions about getting into show business?

D. Start telling everyone at school that she and you are best mates and that your auntie really likes her?

7. You've broken your leg. Your friend comes to visit and:

A. Is really nice and sympathetic – she even brings you a bar of your favourite chocolate and a funny video to help you pass the time?

B. Tells you to stop making such a big deal of it – she was once in a complete body-cast for over two months?

C. Writes loads of embarrassing stuff all over your cast?

D. She doesn't come and visit!

8. You've been admiring your friend's necklace. On your birthday, does your friend:

A. Give you her necklace – if you like it, it must be pretty unfashionable?

B. Give you another necklace, similar but not as nice?

C. Give you an exploding cake – who wants a stupid necklace anyway?

D. Give you her necklace? She tried to buy you one the same, but they don't sell them any more so she's giving you hers instead.

9. Which three words best describe your friend?

A. Funny, wild, impulsive.

B. Considerate, intuitive, generous.

C. Trendy, fickle, selfish.
D. Tough, focused, driven.

10. In a crisis this friend can always be relied upon to:
A. Make you see the funny side.
B. Make you realize it's all your fault.
C. Make like an egg … and beat it.
D. Stick with you.

Now add up your scores:
1. A.8 B.4 C.2 D.6   2. A.6 B.2 C.4 D.8
3. A.4 B.8 C.6 D.2   4. A.4 B.8 C.6 D.2
5. A.8 B.4 C.6 D.2   6. A.4 B.8 C.6 D.2
7. A.8 B.4 C.6 D.2   8. A.2 B.4 C.6 D.8
9. A.6 B.8 C.2 D.4   10. A.6 B.4 C.2 D.8

Note: There are no key words given as this quiz is a reflection on your friends.

71–80 Debbie Dependable
What a diamond girl! This mate is amazing. She's kind, thoughtful, caring and generous to a fault. She knows the value of friendship and she's prepared to put herself out for her friends. Don't take advantage of her good nature, though, you don't want to treat her like Debbie Doormat. She's a good friend to you, so treat her in the way she deserves – that is, basically in exactly the same way she treats you! You're a lucky gal to have a pal like Debs. She's a star!

51–70 Lucy Loud
This girl's out for one thing and one thing only … fun with a capital 'F'! She's loud and she's proud and she doesn't care who knows it. She's just perfect for when you're feeling down in the dumps, as you can't stay blue for long with Lucy Loud around. The only downside is that she just doesn't know how to be serious, so don't look to her for a heavy heart-to-heart – that's just not her scene. But she's funny and

generous and highly addictive. So if you're looking for a good old-fashioned dose of laughter therapy, you couldn't have a better buddy than lovely Lucy Loud!

36–50 Carla Competitive

Missy Carla's got a competitive streak a mile wide. She doesn't mean to be quite as hard-hearted as she sometimes appears, it's just that she finds it hard to believe she's ever second best at anything. Given the opportunity she can be really nice, but she tends to see everyone as a potential threat. A bit of healthy competition is no bad thing and it can keep you on your toes. Just watch out, though, that it isn't all that's going on between you and that underneath you really do care about each other too. You never know, when she realizes that there's plenty of room in this big wide world for more than just her to do well, she might mellow and become a mate in a million.

20–35 Shallow Suzie

Hmmm, this girl's always got her eye on the next big chance. She's talking to you, but she's looking over your shoulder to see if someone more interesting is coming along. She doesn't mean to be hurtful, it's just that she sees herself as one of life's trendsetters and it's a difficult position to maintain. True, she's a bit of a fair-weather friend, but she's very useful for top tips on what's hot and what's not. Stick with her and there'll come a time when she understands that real friends never go out of fashion!

The ★ ★★ Friendship Game ★

A game for two to four players: you will need a dice and one button per person.

Rules

Each person places their button on the start square and rolls the dice. The person who rolls the highest number goes first and then each take turns in a clockwise direction. Roll the dice and move your button the correct number of squares.

Follow the instructions on every challenge square you land on. Each person's go ends when they land on a square without a movement instruction or they have completed their truth / dare. The first person to get to the end is the winner.

If more than two people are playing and you land on a square that asks you something about your mate, always complete the challenge using the friend on your right-hand side.

Truth or dare squares

When you come to a truth or dare square, you have to decide if you'd rather answer a question put by your friend on your right (truthfully, of course) or do a dare! Remember, if you ask nasty questions or set horrible dares the same may happen to you when it's your turn, so try to be nice!

1 **START HERE**	2 Planned a surprise party for your mate's birthday. Go forward 3.	3 Truth or dare
12 Do an impression of a friend from school. If your friend knows who it is go forward 4. If not, go back 2.	11 Truth or dare	10
13	14 Truth or dare	15 What is the date of your friend's birthday? Got it right, go forward 1. Wrong, back 2
24	23 Your mate's got a cold and can't come out sledging so you stay in to keep her company. Go forward 4.	22
25 What's your mate's middle name? Got it right, go forward 2. Wrong, back 1	26 Truth or dare	27

4	**5** Truth or dare	**6** Sing your friend's fave song. Got it right, go forward 1. Wrong, go back 2.
9 u borrow your friend's rrings and lose one. Go ck 5.	**8** Truth or dare	**7**
16	**17** Truth or dare	**18** What's your mate's mum or dad's first name? Right, forward 1. Wrong, back 2.
21 mpletely forgot your ate's birthday. Back to the rt please!	**20** Truth or dare	**19**
28 u borrowed your mate's aths homework and forgot give it back before the son! Go back 9.	**29**	**30** HOORAY! You're a **REALLY GREAT MATE!!!**

SEASONAL SPECIAL

The True Love Test

Write down the name of the boy you fancy

EDMUND DELICATESSENIO

Followed by the word 'loves'

LOVES

And then your name

SYLVIA CHRYSANTHEMUM

Now go through each letter in the word 'LOVES' and see how many times it appears in your two names. So, in my example:

L   O   V   E   S
2   1   1   5   4

(There are two Ls in our couple's names: one in Sylvia and one in Delicatessenio. There is one O: at the end of Delicatessenio. And so on.)

Now add each of these numbers together as shown by the arrows. So:

2 + 1 + 1 + 5 + 4
3 + 2 + 6 + 9
5 + 8 + 15
13 + 23

Keep adding the numbers together until you have two lots left. Now add these two together to get your true love score!

Edmund's and Sylvia's chances of true and ever-lasting love come out at a healthy **36%**

Not bad for old Ed and Sylv then, but what's it like for you?

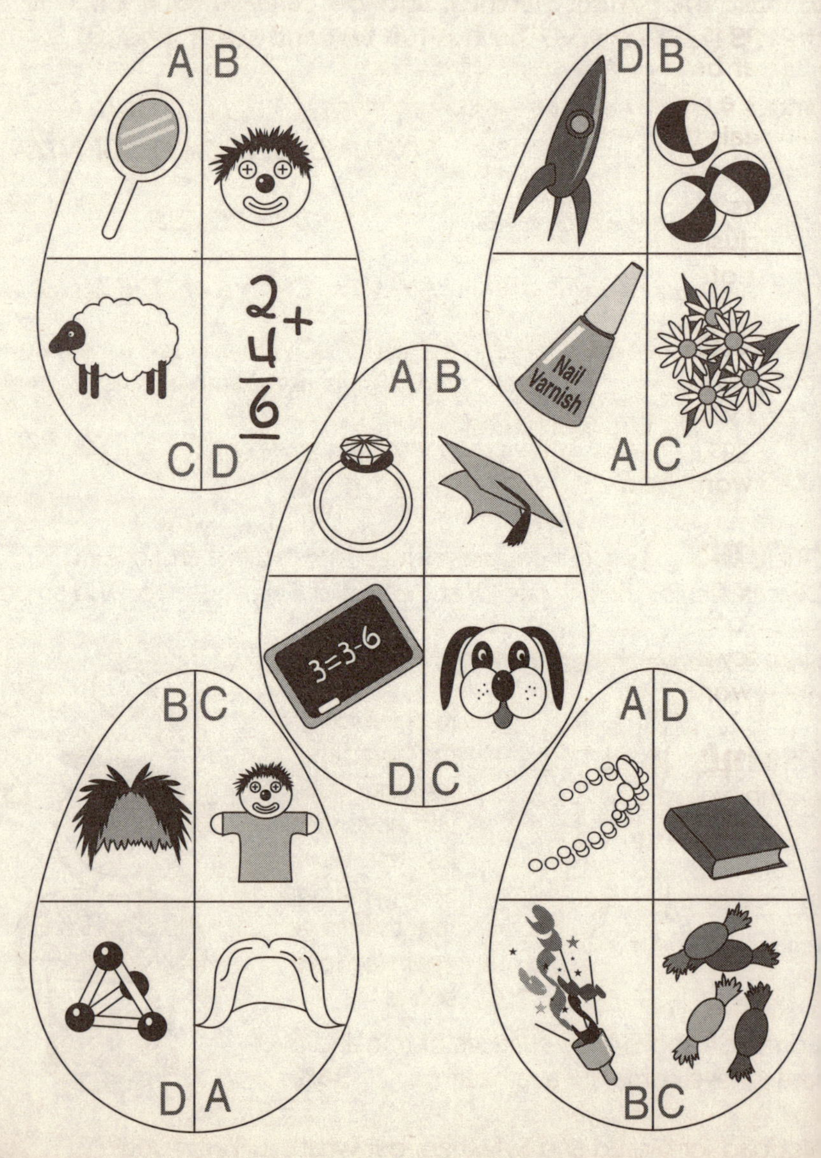

Feature

Spring is in the air, but are you a bonny Easter bonnet or a mad March hare? Make a note of the picture that most appeals to you in each of the Easter eggs on the left. Then count up the letters that you chose and read the conclusion for the one you picked most of.

Mainly 'A's: Easter Bonnet

You like making yourself look pretty, but you don't want to get chocolate on your nice dress. No eggs for you!
Key word: vain

Mainly 'B's: Mad March Hare

You're bouncy and you're bonkers, but you give everyone a great laugh so that's just fine. Five choccy eggs for you, bunny!
Key word: mad

Mainly 'C's: Fluffy Chick

Ahhh, you're a bit of a baby at heart. You like to be looked after and you're a total softie when it comes to anything furry or fluffy. Three ickle eggs for you.
Key word: soppy

Mainly 'D's: Egg Head

You're a bit of a brainiac, aren't you? Have some chocolate brain food – four eggs for you!
Key word: brainy

CHRISTMAS STAR

Are you an Ebenezer Scrooge or Santa's little helper? Climb the tree to find out! Start in the tub at the bottom of the tree and, answering the questions at each level, see how far you get! The answers are on the next page.

You're a real Christmas star – you love everything about Christmas and want to make it as nice for everyone as possible. Shine on, girl!

The big morning's arrived. Do you:

A. Leap out of bed and run round the house seeing what everyone got in their stocking?

B. Roll over and try to go back to sleep? You've opened your stocking already.

It's time to decorate the tree. Do you:

A. Take your time making it look really special?

B. Work your way through the box as quickly as possible?

When you buy your Christmas presents, do you:

A. Think really hard about what each person would like?

B. Go to your local jumble sale and spend as little as possible?

When it comes to Christmas dinner:

A. It's just about your favourite meal of the whole year.

B. You hate absolutely everything about it.

Your mum asks you to help wrap your sister's presents. Do you think:

A. Yippee – you love wrapping pressies and making them look as nice as possible?

B. Boring – wrapping your own stuff was enough of a chore?

When you think of Christmas, do you feel:

A. Depressed? All that money I have to spend, all that shopping I have to do.

B. Excited? All those pressies, all that lovely food – you just love it all!

START HERE

Answers

A. You're a
real Christmas
treat – up you go!
B. Well, you can just stay in
bed until New Year as far as I'm
concerned – naughty!

A. I can see it now –
beautiful. Go on up!
B. You've got a little over-excited.
You're going to have to stay here until
you calm down. Sorry!

A. You're such a nice person
– move on up.
B. Back down that tree, babe, you've blown it!

A. Move up to the next layer – if
you're not too full to make it.
B. You'd done OK up to now, but let's face it,
Christmas dinner *is* Christmas. Go no further.

A. That's the spirit
– move on up
B. Stop right there,
Scroogy.

A. Off to a bad start – get off the tree
and skip Christmas altogether.
B. Up you go!

What Season Are You?

Do you thrive in the warmth of the golden summer sun? Do you suit the rich colours of autumn leaves? Is it the cold, clean winter snow that inspires you? Or is it in spring that you really do your thing? Now's your chance to find out!

Read each list and note down on a piece of paper the one thing that most appeals to you out of each set of four. Don't spend time thinking about it, just let your instincts guide you.

 ice lolly

 pumpkin

 Christmas pudding

 Easter egg

 the smell of fallen leaves

 the smell of roasting chestnuts

 the smell of coconut

 the smell of fuchsias

 white

 yellow

 orange and red

 pink and lilac

 purple and gold

 green

 blue

 brown

 bumble bee

 rabbit

 reindeer

 black cat

 robin redbreast

 blue tit

 swallow

 pheasant

 firework

 sandcastle

 snowman

 daffodil

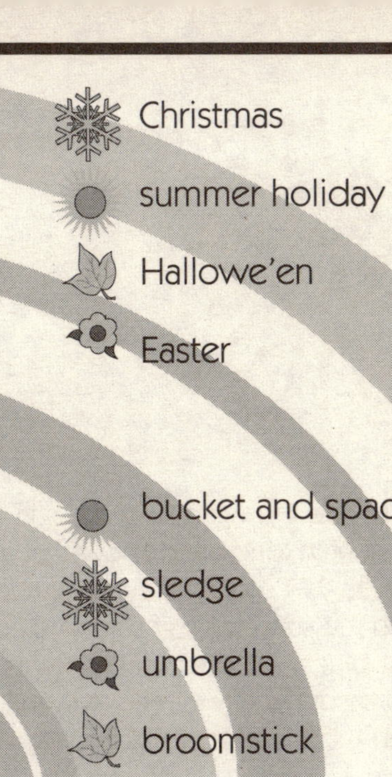

Now count how many of each symbol you chose and read the conclusion under the one you had the most of.

Summer Sunshine

You like nothing better than to feel the warmth of the sun on your face, breathe in the smell of suntan lotion and know that all is right with the world. You love the bright colours of summer and the noise of people having fun in the sun. You suit sunshine colours – glowing yellows and brilliant blues – and you feel alive as soon as the sun comes out. Like the season, you're cheery and fun and love to shine on those around you – but be careful not to let your light fade when the sun's no longer around.

Key word: warm

Autumn Leaves

You love the crisp, sharp days of autumn. Your idea of heaven is kicking through the fallen leaves, breathing in the damp scent of the year grown old. You suit autumn colours – burnt coppers, bronzes and rich chestnut browns. You love the thrill of Hallowe'en and the excitement of bonfire night. You're like the season, fresh and breezy, but with a smouldering wild side that could explode at any minute!

Key word: breezy

Winter Snowflakes

You like the cold, fresh days of winter. You love the bracing air and the way it contrasts with the cosy warmth of home. You look forward to Christmas as one of the highlights of your year. You suit winter colours, deep crimsons and regal purples. You love bundling up in winter woollies and seeing your breath in the air. Like the season, you have two sides: you can sometimes appear cool, but that's only on the outside; inside, you're as warming as a hot toddy and as loving and giving as any Christmas morning!

Key word: fresh

Spring Flowers

You love the awakening of the new year. The fresh air and the earth bursting with new life fills you with optimism and a sense of well-being. You love spring colours – pastel pinks, lilacs and greens. Like the season, you're changeable – always growing and looking for the next thing to take your interest. You're like a breath of fresh air after a long dark winter!

Key word: optimistic

Delve Deeper

In this section you get to explore the inner you and some dimensions of your personality that you might not have looked at before. But remember, don't get seriously spooked – it's really just for fun!

The Future's Yours

Want a fun way to find out what might be in store for you in the future? Try the following test and you never know, some of it might even come true!

On a piece of paper write down the following:

1. The colour you are most drawn to:
   red, pink, blue, yellow or green.
2. A number.
3. The names of three of your girlfriends.
4. A month in the year.
5. A place.
6. A boy's name.

Now have a look at what destiny might hold!

1. A parcel wrapped in this colour paper could bring you peace of mind.
2. It is this many days until you might meet a person who will give you some good advice.
3. The first person is the one you care most about, the second is the person who cares most about you and the third person will go up in your estimation.
4. In this month something might happen that you will not like, but it will turn out for the best in the end.
5. If you picked somewhere close to home, expect an unexpected visitor. If you picked somewhere far away, you will be going on an unexpected trip quite soon.
6. A boy of this name could bring you some exciting news.

How Psychic Are You?

If you've ever had the uncanny feeling that you've been somewhere before, or know just exactly what your friend is going to say before she even opens her mouth to say it, you could be psychic! In which case, you probably already know how you're going to score on this quiz … Well, let's see if you're right!

1. When you have a vivid dream, do you:
A. Expect it to come true – it happens all the time?
B. Not really expect it to come true, but if it did, once in a while, you wouldn't be that surprised?
C. Not expect it to come true and you'd be surprised if it did?
D. Know it won't come true – they never do?

2. How often do you experience déjà vu (when you suddenly get the feeling you've seen or done something before):
A. All the time?
B. Not very often?
C. Hardly ever?
D. Never?

3. You're thinking about someone you haven't seen / heard from for ages and the next minute you get a letter / phone call from them. Are you:
A. Not at all surprised – it was obviously meant to happen?
B. A little surprised?
C. Amazed – that's really weird?
D. It wouldn't happen to me!

4. Have you ever seen a ghost?
A. Yes.
B. I thought so, but now I'm not sure …
C. No.
D. I don't believe in them, so how can I see something which doesn't exist?

Now add up your psychic subscores:
1. A.20 B.15 C.10 D.5   2. A.20 B.15 C.10 D.5
3. A.20 B.15 C.10 D.5   4. A.20 B.15 C.10 D.5

Add together your scores to get your first psychic subscore.

Now go on and do the following tests.

5. Get your friend to give you something from a place she's visited or been on holiday to – a postcard or small souvenir will do. Make sure she hasn't told you anything about the place before and that she doesn't tell you anything about it until you've completed your experiment.

Hold on to the object and stare hard at it. See what images of the place your friend went to come into your mind and note them down on a piece of paper. Then check with your friend how many aspects of her holiday destination you got right! Remember, she's not allowed to prompt you in any way, so try standing with your back to her when you speak to make sure that she can't even visually signal when you've got something right.

How many aspects did you get right:

A. Over ten?
B. Over five?
C. Fewer than five?
D. I didn't get anything right!

6. Make yourself a set of mind-reading cards. Pick four simple shapes (a star, a heart, a diamond and waves, for example) and draw them out a number of times on a piece of paper. Cut them out into cards.

Get a friend to sit behind you with the cards and concentrate on them one at a time. As she holds each card, try to guess what shape she's thinking of. Get your friend to note down how many you get right. Chances are that you'll guess the right shape half the time. So if you guess your friend's cards more than half the time (eg, more than five out of every ten cards), you might be psychic!

Did you get:
A. The right image less than 60 per cent of the time?
B. The right image more than 60 per cent of the time?

7. Ask a friend to give you a favourite object of theirs (a teddy, a picture, an item of clothing). Hold it quietly for a while and see what images come into your head. Can you tell where they got it from or who gave it to them? Say whatever comes into your head. It may not be immediately obvious to you why it would have anything to do with that particular object. Get your friend to make a note of how many things you get right.

Did you get:
A. Over ten?
B. Over five?
C. Fewer than five?
D. I didn't get anything!

Now add up your psychic subscores:
5. A.20 B.15 C.10 D.5   6. A.10   B.20
7. A.20 B.15 C.10 D.5

Add together your scores to get your second psychic subscore.

8. Look at the following lists and pick the word (A, B, C or D) that you feel goes best with the first word. Work on instinct, so do it really quickly without thinking about it.

1. Travel
A. exploration   B. journey   C. discovery   D. visit

2. Love
A. marriage   B. giving   C. need   D. for ever

3. Hold
A. hands   B. trapped   C. secure   D. warmth

4. Stretch
A. expand   B. exercise   C. reach   D. touch

5. Imagine
A. brain   B. dreams   C. reality   D. desire

Now add up your psychic subscores:
1. A.15 B.10 C.20 D.5   2. A.5   B.15 C.10 D.20
3. A.5   B.10 C.15 D.20   4. A.15 B.5   C.10 D.20
5. A.5   B.15 C.10 D.20

Add together these scores for your third psychic subscore. Then add all your three psychic subscores together to give you your final psychic rating!

181–240 Follow Your Instincts
Wow! Your sixth-sense antenna is in constant tingle mode. You're not about to start telling the future or anything drastic like that, but you are very switched on to what's happening around you. You pick up on all sorts of signals without even realizing it. You are open to impressions that simply wash over other people.
Key word: instinctive

121–180 Get Connected
You're very intuitively in tune. You pick up on the vibes other people give off and know how to read them. You have particularly good connections with those close to you and often know how they're feeling or what they're thinking without being told.
Key word: connected

81–120 Sensitive Soul

You believe that there are some strange things that go on in the world that seem to defy explanation, but you're not really going to lose sleep over them. You are ruled more by your emotions than Ms Logic, but you're not going to let your heart lead your head entirely. In fact, you like to balance up the two before making an informed decision.

Key word: sensitive

65–80 Miss Logic

As far as you're concerned, there's a logical explanation for everything. Your brain is as sharp as a new pin, but only in the pursuit of facts and figures to support your theories for explaining the unexplainable. You certainly aren't afraid of any silly old ghosts … because as far as you're concerned they don't even exist!

Key word: logical

Dangle Power

If you want a fun way to find the answer to some of life's less-important questions, why not try a spot of dangling! Some people think pendulum power's a great way to get answers to the questions that have been bugging them for ages. Using a swinging object to find out something is actually called 'dowsing', and you can have a go at it too!

Make a pendulum by threading a key or a ring on to a piece of cotton. Think of a fun question you really want answering, like 'Should I lend my little sister my favourite pen?' or 'Should I phone my best friend?' Hold the thread of your pendulum between your forefinger and thumb about seven centimetres above the weight. Let it swing over the chart on the next page. Wait for a minute or so until the swing is really definite. The answer it swings over is the one for you. Cool!

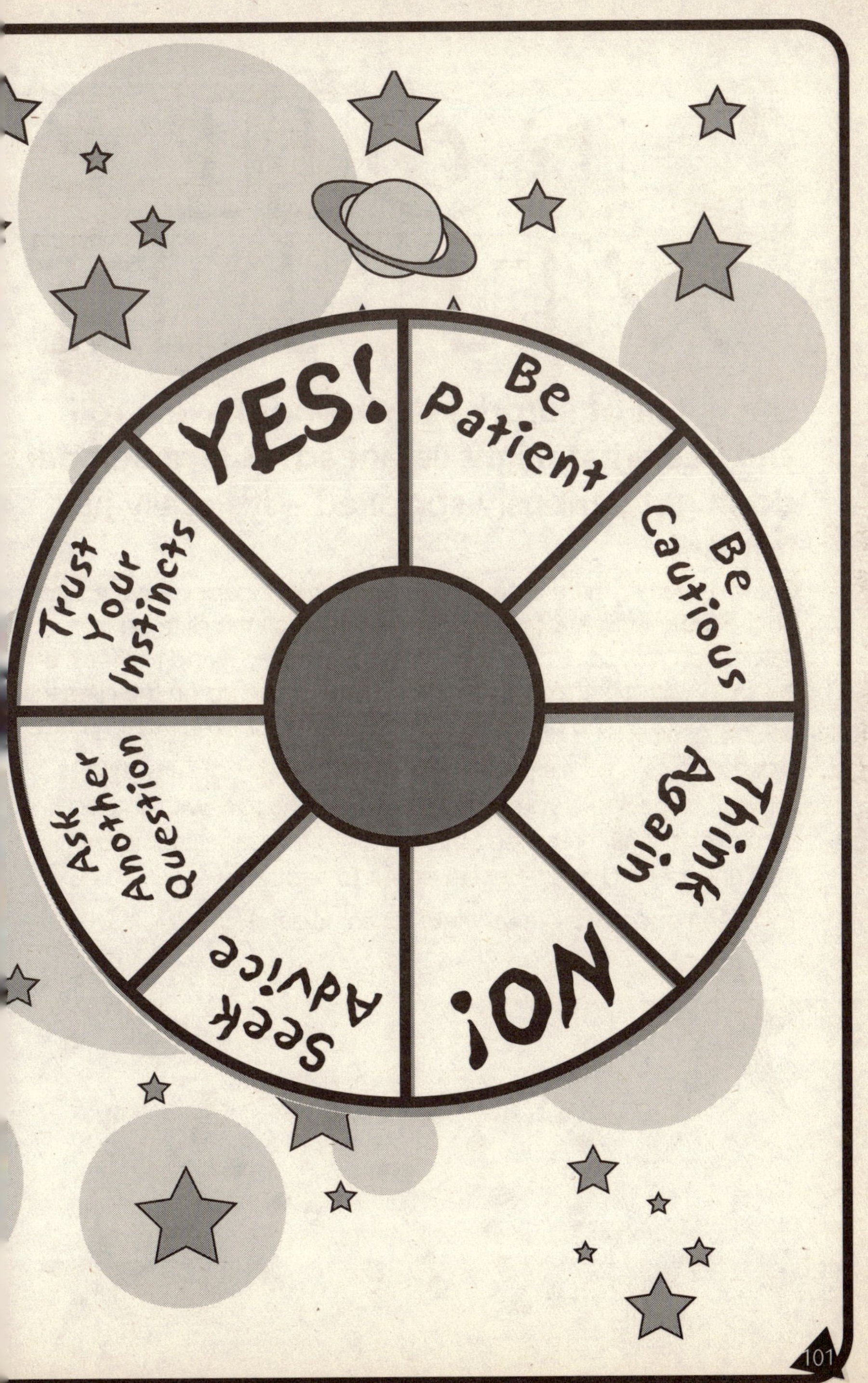
YES!
Be Patient
Be Cautious
Trust Your Instincts
Think Again
Ask Another Question
¡NO!
Seek Advice

Life is full of surprises! Why not have a roll and see what might lie ahead? But remember, don't get seriously spooked – it's really just for fun!

Gather together three dice and an A4 piece of paper. Put the paper on the table in front of you and prepare to roll the dice on to it. Before you roll, say to the dice, 'What lies ahead?' and roll for the answer. Add together the numbers that are face up on the dice that have landed on the paper and read the conclusion for that number.

If one dice falls off the paper you might get a bit of surprising news. If two fall off, you could have a bit of a row with a good friend. And if all three don't make it on to the paper, something truly unexpected might be just about to happen!

Try rolling once every few weeks for an update!

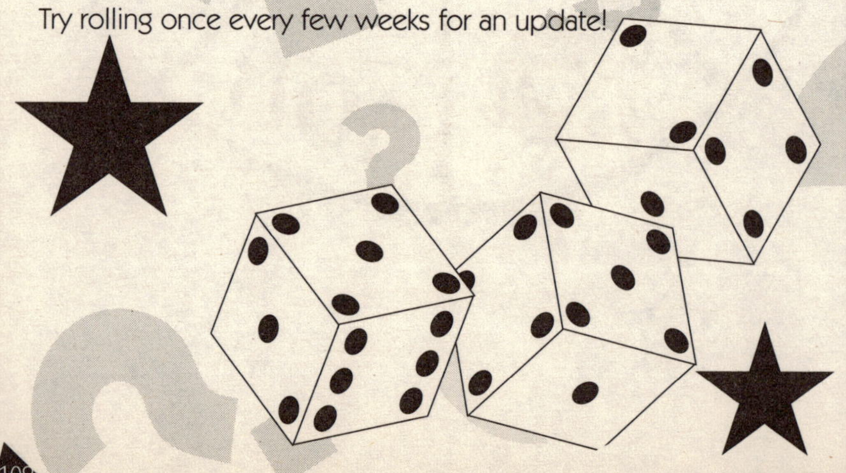

1. You could find out that someone's been talking about you.

2. You might make up with a friend you fell out with a long time ago.

3. You might get the blame for something you didn't do.

4. There could be some money coming your way.

5. You're in for a run of good luck.

6. You might get caught out over a little fib you've told.

7. You're going to get your way over something.

8. You might make a new friend.

9. A letter could be coming your way.

10. You might find something you thought you'd lost.

11. You could be short of cash.

12. You're going to succeed at something.

13. You might get given some bad advice – ignore it!

14. You're heading for a really happy and carefree time.

15. You could get a nice gift.

16. You might receive some happy news.

17. Things could be looking up for you.

18. You might see someone you haven't thought about for a while.

We've Got Your Number

Some people believe that the time and date you were born can have an influence on the type of person you are. Your character, personality and even your outlook on life can be worked out from the numbers in your birthday! Have a go at this fun numbers game and see just what sort of person you might add up to!

Write out all the numbers in your date of birth (counting only the last two digits of the year) and add them together from the left to the right. For example, if you were born on 24 August 1988, write out:

$$2 + 4 + 8 + 8 + 8 = 30$$

Then add these two numbers together, so:

$$3 + 0 = 3$$

(If at this stage you still have a two-digit number, add them together again.)

The single number you are left with is the one that will reveal all!

1 Lead On!

You're an independent type and you rather like to get your own way. You're hard-working and full of bright ideas, and you are prepared to do whatever it takes to see them through. You can be a bit of a perfectionist, which can sometimes make you critical of those less able than yourself. Also, you have difficulty in taking criticism from other people – as far as you're concerned, you're always right! The perfect career for you would be in politics. Fancy yourself as prime minister?

Key word: leader

2 The Go-between

You're a right one for pouring oil on troubled waters. You hate any sort of trouble and if your friends fall out, it's always you who's the peace-keeper. You are quite sensitive and have a good instinct for people. Your friends can often treat you as the resident agony aunt, as they know you'll be prepared to listen and can give good advice. The perfect career for you would be as an international diplomat.

Key word: diplomat

3 The Show Girl

You're a bit of a performer at heart. You love the limelight and like nothing better than keeping your friends entertained. When something fires your imagination, you go for it with gusto and your enthusiasm is often contagious. You're quite a cheerful soul and even when you're feeling down you try to bluster your way through. Career wise? Well, it's got to be the stage for you.

Key word: performer

4 The Loyal Plodder

Believe me, it's not as bad as it sounds! You're a really hard worker. You're logical and methodical and like to take your time getting things right. But you won't cut corners and you are incredibly reliable. If you say you'll do something, it's as good as done, and it's done really well. You never let your friends down and you're as loyal as the day is long. Landscape gardening could be a good career move for you.

Key word: loyal

5 The Jack of All Trades

You change your mind as often as most people change their socks! You're good at lots of different things and pick new things up very easily. The trouble is that you become bored very easily too, so it's only a matter of time before you tire of your latest skill and move on to something else. There may not be only one career choice for you – you might want to try a few – but as you're naturally quite inquisitive and like a bit of adventure, a journalist or foreign correspondent might be the job for you.

Key word: multi-talented

6 The Teacher Creature

You're a bit of a brainiac without being a boring boffin. You like to share what you know and can make it interesting for others. You have an inquiring mind and enjoy finding stuff out. You're enthusiastic and like to motivate others too. You're also a good judge of character and stay quite calm in a crisis. Career prospects? Looks like you could be going back to school!

Key word: wise

7 The Indie Girl

You really do enjoy your own company. You have the courage of your convictions and don't feel the need for approval from other people. You have quite a developed spiritual side and sometimes just like to sit quietly, lost in your own thoughts. You'll be quite happy in some kind of self-employment, as you don't need to feel part of a team in order to get on. Ideal career path – writer, artist or vicar, of course!

Key words: independent

8 The Go-getter

Blimey, slow down, will you! You love organizing stuff and getting things done. You're the same with people too: you like to help them to get the best out of themselves and encourage them to do well. In fact, you're a regular Little Miss Motivator! You're determined and responsible and would make a good managing director of a multinational corporation – phew!

Key word: ambitious

9 The Carer

You're quite a deep thinker, especially about the big questions in life. You have a tendency to carry all the worries of the world on your shoulders, but then you can also be very motivated. When you feel passionate about something, you have no problem at all inspiring others. You could use this skill in being a very successful fund-raiser for a struggling charity.

Key word: caring

The Write Stuff

What secrets does your handwriting reveal about the type of person you are? The analysis of handwriting is known as graphology. People have been studying handwriting for hundreds of years to try to unravel aspects of the writer's personality.

On a piece of paper write about three sentences in your normal handwriting. Don't copy from anything, just write quickly off the top of your head. Now take a look at what your handwriting says about you.

1. **Look at the sample handwriting on the next page. Which is most similar to yours? Don't worry if they aren't exactly the same as yours, just find the one that you feel is the closest.**

A *A Sample of handwriting*

B *A sample of handwriting*

C *A sample of handwriting*

D *A sample of handwriting*

2. **Do you use heavy or light pressure when writing (check this by turning the page over to see if you've caused the paper to become raised on the other side – if you have, you use a heavy pressure when writing)?**
A. Light.
B. Heavy.

3. **Do you prefer to write with a thick or a thin pen:**
A. Thick.
B. Thin.

4. Do you join your letters up:
A. Throughout your writing?
B. Some of the time?
C. Never?

5. Is your writing:
A. Short and wide?
B. Tall and thin?
C: Neither of the above?

6. Is your writing:
A. Neat?
B. Messy?

7. Now write your signature on your piece of paper. Which style does it most resemble:
A. Small, neat and legible?
B. Illegible?
C. Loopy and flowery?
D. Curvy and clear?

Using the chart on the next page, match up your answers to the correct conclusions. Make a note of all the conclusion boxes you chose to get an overall picture.

Some of your conclusions may seem to contradict each other, but that's quite normal. Your personality is very complex and you have a lot of different sides to your character, so your handwriting will simply reflect that fact.

Your key words are highlighted in bold throughout.

1

A. You're an **imaginative** type and your mind is always dotting around from one idea to the next. You like to try out a different hobby a week and can get bored easily. You'll always succeed in the artistic side of life.

B. You're a very focused person. Once you set your mind on something, you can guarantee it will get done. But you can be a bit **inflexible**. You like to have everything planned out and you hate surprises.

C. You can be a bit of a **shy** girl and take your time in picking your friends. But when you do, you're ever so loyal, so it looks like they've got a friend for life!

D. You're a **happy-go-lucky** kind of girl. You're outgoing and cheerful and find it pretty easy to make friends. You're enthusiastic and full of bounce and people can get tired just looking at you!

2

A. You're an **adaptable** type, more than happy to go with the flow. You are considerate and kind and friendly too!

B. You're energetic and **impulsive**. You often act before you think. You are practical and adventurous with a bit of a competitive streak.

3

A. You're **sociable** and generally good fun to be with. You are cheerful and like trying new things. You're pretty confident and like anything that's a bit on the arty side.

B. You're a bit of a **deep thinker**. You pick your friends quite carefully and enjoy spending time on your own or with just a couple of other people who you really care about.

4

A. You like to stick to a routine. You're very **self-disciplined** and certainly not afraid of hard work. But sometimes you need to learn to lighten up a little!

B. You have a wonderful balance between your head and your heart. You're good with your hands, **practical** and caring.

C. You're a **spontaneous** type – you act on instinct and think later. You love to travel and see new things.

5

A. You're an **outgoing** optimist – friendly, lively and sympathetic to other people's needs. In fact, you're a great person to have around!

B. You're a bit of a **perfectionist**. You tend to focus on one thing and go for it with all your heart. You are often good at maths or the sciences and like to keep yourself to yourself.

C. You have quite a mature outlook on life. You're **hard-working** but flexible and you like being part of a team. You fit in well and are prepared to compromise when necessary.

6

A. You are a **calm** and reliable person. You like to be part of a team and enjoy making plans.

B. You are adventurous and **enthusiastic**. You like to take life as it comes and are full of surprises.

7

A. You are **well-organized** and well-behaved. You're quite cautious and don't tend to leap in before thinking things through. You believe there is a time and a place for everything and, fortunately for your friends, that does include having a laugh – phew!

B. Your signature, being hard to read, is representative of you! You like to keep what you're thinking to yourself and sometimes appear as quite **aloof** and mysterious. But actually you have a softer side – you just don't always like to show it.

C. You're a real people person. You like to hang out in a crowd and you're good at getting on with other people. You are **imaginative**, with a flair for the artistic – but watch out, you can be just a bit slushy at times!

D. You are affectionate and sensitive to other people's needs. You're a **great listener** and good at giving advice. I see a career as an agony aunt looming!

A Room with a View

Is your bedroom full of good karma or bursting with bad vibes? According to feng shui, the ancient Chinese discipline, if you sort your stuff out in just the right way it can improve your luck and have a really good influence on your future. What you have in your room and where you put it can affect your destiny. So take the test and see if you're in feng shui heaven or not.

Read the passage below. Three symbols appear throughout in groups of related sentences. Every time something is mentioned that is true for your room, note down the symbol used on a separate piece of paper. At the end, count up how many of each of the symbols you have and read the conclusion for the symbol you have most of.

When you come into my room the first thing you notice are all the lovely bright colours / are one or two bright things / is that it's not very colourful.

I love the mirror I have on the wall. As you walk in, it is right opposite the door. I don't have a mirror on my wall.

I have just been to the market and bought flowers for my room.
I will put them on the window sill to improve the view.
I didn't buy anything – flowers give me hay fever!

My room looks out on to a brick wall / busy road / a small
garden / a big garden or a field with lots of trees in the
distance.

It's really time I tidied up. My room is so messy / a bit on the
cluttered side / has only one or two things out of place,
other than that it's as neat as a new pin.

I love all my pictures and posters. I have lots of them. Some
are of people and some are of places I would love to go.
I don't like anything on my walls.

I just have one central light in my room. I don't really feel the need
for any more. I have a couple of lights. I like lots of little
lights all around my room.

I'd better get some work done now. My desk is nice and neat.
My desk is a bit messy but I can find everything I need.
My desk is really messy … now where did I put that ruler?

I'm exhausted now – time to hit the sack! My bed is against the wall
where there is no window or door / not facing the door /
facing the door.

I have lots of lovely soft furnishings in my room – a throw on my bed and big cushions . I don't have many soft furnishings, but I have one or two . I have lots of angular furniture  .

My bed is crammed in the corner. I find it really cosy that way . My bed only has one side touching a wall . My bed has all around it and I sleep like a top . Goodnight!

Dragon

The Dragon is one of the signs of the Chinese zodiac and the most powerful symbol of good luck, and that's just what you've got. Mirrors are very important in feng shui. They brighten up a room by reflecting light and can make it look bigger. They're also great for catching or deflecting bad vibes – apparently! Bright colours are cheery and good for lifting the spirits, and flowers and plants bring elements of the natural world into your room. Lights are also warming and will help keep a happy atmosphere, and pictures of your favourite people and places will prove really inspirational to you. Keeping your room tidy, as you seem to do, makes your life much easier. You know where everything is and so can get things done much more quickly and with little stress. It sounds like you've got feng shui well and truly sorted.

Key word: effective

Goldfish

You're nearly there. Some things are hard to change, like where you can fit the bed or what the view's like out of the window. But it's not hard to improve them. Always leave a space around your bed so the good energy can circulate easily, and save up for a nice bright throw if your old duvet cover's getting a bit dull. If you like having fresh flowers in your room, try putting them on the window sill as this will soften the view. Why not get a wind-chime too – the sound is really soothing? I can feel those vibes improving already!

Key word: improving

Rubbish Bin

Oh dear. Sounds like your room needs a good-vibe spring-clean! Tidying up might be a good start. It's hard to feel happy and relaxed when you're surrounded by a week's worth of dirty knickers. Once you've cleared some space, you'll be able to see more easily what you could make of your room. Get some posters and arrange them in a nice pattern on the wall. Clear up your desk … you could buy some cheap storage containers to keep your stuff in – metal is a very lucky element in feng shui, so get yourself some cute tins. I bet it's looking better already. Other ideas you might like to try are getting yourself a couple of mirrors (look in second-hand shops for some real bargains) and a little bedside lamp for some mood lighting (again second-hand shops often have some funky little numbers going very cheap). Before you know it, your room will be feng shui magic and bursting at the seams with really good vibes!

Key word: messy

DREAM BELIEVER

Ever had that dream where you're dressed in a giant bunny suit, cooking pancakes, while your best friend floats over your head in an armchair? No? Me neither! But if you did, you could be sure there might just be some hidden meaning there – like you love rabbits, adore pancakes and think your friend's just a bit over the top!

Dreams are a way we have of dealing with stuff we don't, or can't, get around to dealing with in the day. Check out this quiz and see what your subconscious is saying about you.

Look at all the dreams below and then make a note of any you have had recently. Count up how many of each symbol you have and then read the conclusion for the symbol you have most of.

I've recently dreamt about:

 an accident

 floating against the current

 having aching arms and legs

 freedom

 performing badly in a play / show

 performing well in a play / show

fleeing / running away
an approaching hurricane
seeing an ambulance
horses
apes
missing an appointment
Travel to faraway places
baking
admiring others
You're a bandit
having a bath
sun-drenched beach
a beautiful woman
birthday
book
a returning boomerang
cooking
lending to a friend
being chased
fluffy white clouds
someone (not you) committing a crime
cleaning a room
the devil
rescuing a drowning person
sitting around a fire with others
staring eyes
pointing fingers

 blue  brown  red  yellow  green

Success Seeker

You feel like you're on the brink of something big. You've got the feeling you're about to succeed in something and it's coming through into your dreams. Some of your dreams are fairly obvious symbols of prosperity and success, such as travel, exotic locations and performing well in a play. Others, though, are less obvious. If you noted down admiring others, it isn't because you're jealous of them, but more because you see them being where you will soon be yourself. If you dream of books, it means that you are well-behaved on the whole and also that you believe that study will lead to success and financial reward. All in all, your dreams are leading you in one direction only … and that's up!

Key word: successful

Put Upon

Hmmm, you're feeling a bit downtrodden at the moment. Maybe your mates are always turning to you for advice and you feel like you don't get a lot of consideration back in return. Some of your dreams are fairly obvious symbols of this feeling: rescuing a drowning person, lending things to a friend and trying to float against the current all represent quite clearly the feeling of carrying weight upon your shoulders. Some of your dreams aren't so obvious, though. Apes signify that you worry people are taking advantage of your good nature. Dreaming of freedom is a wish-fulfilment dream – in other words, it's how you'd ideally like to be, free of everyone else's problems!

Try making it clear that you're not just around to listen to everyone else's problems in your waking life and I'm sure you'll soon be having the sweetest dreams around!
Key words: weighed down

Stressed Out

Uh-oh, potential anxiety attack coming on! You're a bit of a worry-guts and it comes over in the dreams you have. You might just worry about little things in life, like whether you remembered to give your mum your dirty games kit or not, but because you're a worrier these translate into major disasters in your dreams. That's why you're dreaming of approaching hurricanes, being chased and speeding ambulances. But remember, this isn't necessarily a bad thing. By dealing with your daytime anxieties in your dreams, you may well be sorting them out before you even wake up, so you'll have less to worry about during the day! Clever, eh?
Key word: worrier

Happy

Well, you seem pretty contented with your lot. You get on with your family, have good friends and are pretty happy with your life all round, which is nice! A lot of your dreams are quite obviously symbolic of this contented feeling: fluffy white clouds and sitting round the fire with good company speak for themselves. Cooking is also a homely event, symbolizing family and security. As for dreaming about having aching arms and legs, that's symbolic of the sort of contented feeling you can have after a hard day's work well done. Sounds like you deserve a rest … You'd better go back to bed and get some more sleep!
Key word: contented

Guilty

Oh dear, you've got a bit of a guilty conscience. It's probably not over anything major – I doubt you've robbed any banks lately! – but whatever it is, your subconscious mind is having a little niggle at you about it. You've probably just borrowed a top from your sister and spilt blackcurrant down it, or told a tiny little white lie to a friend, so don't get too bent out of shape about it. Your dreams fall into two categories: those symbolizing the actual guilty feeling – being a bandit and pointing fingers – and the others representing your desire to shake off the guilty feeling by running away or washing it away. But don't worry too much. Remember, your dreams are a way of dealing with things you've got on your mind, so you may well wake up and find you don't feel that guilty after all. And, if it all gets too much for you, you can always confess and face the music. You never know, your sister might not even be that mad at you!

Key word: guilty

Why not try keeping a dream-diary for a few weeks, then come back and have another go. Have your dreams changed?

Colourful Advice

What colour rules your life?

Draw a circle on a piece of paper like the one below. In each section of the circle place a small object of the right colour (it can be as simple as a button). If you haven't got an object for a particular colour, just use a crayon to make a mark in the right colour.

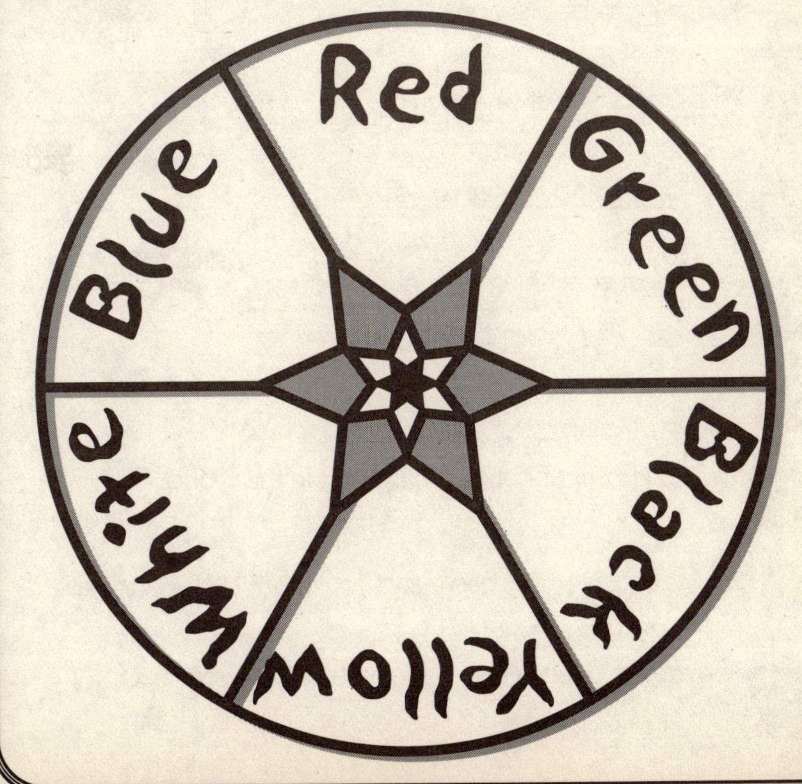

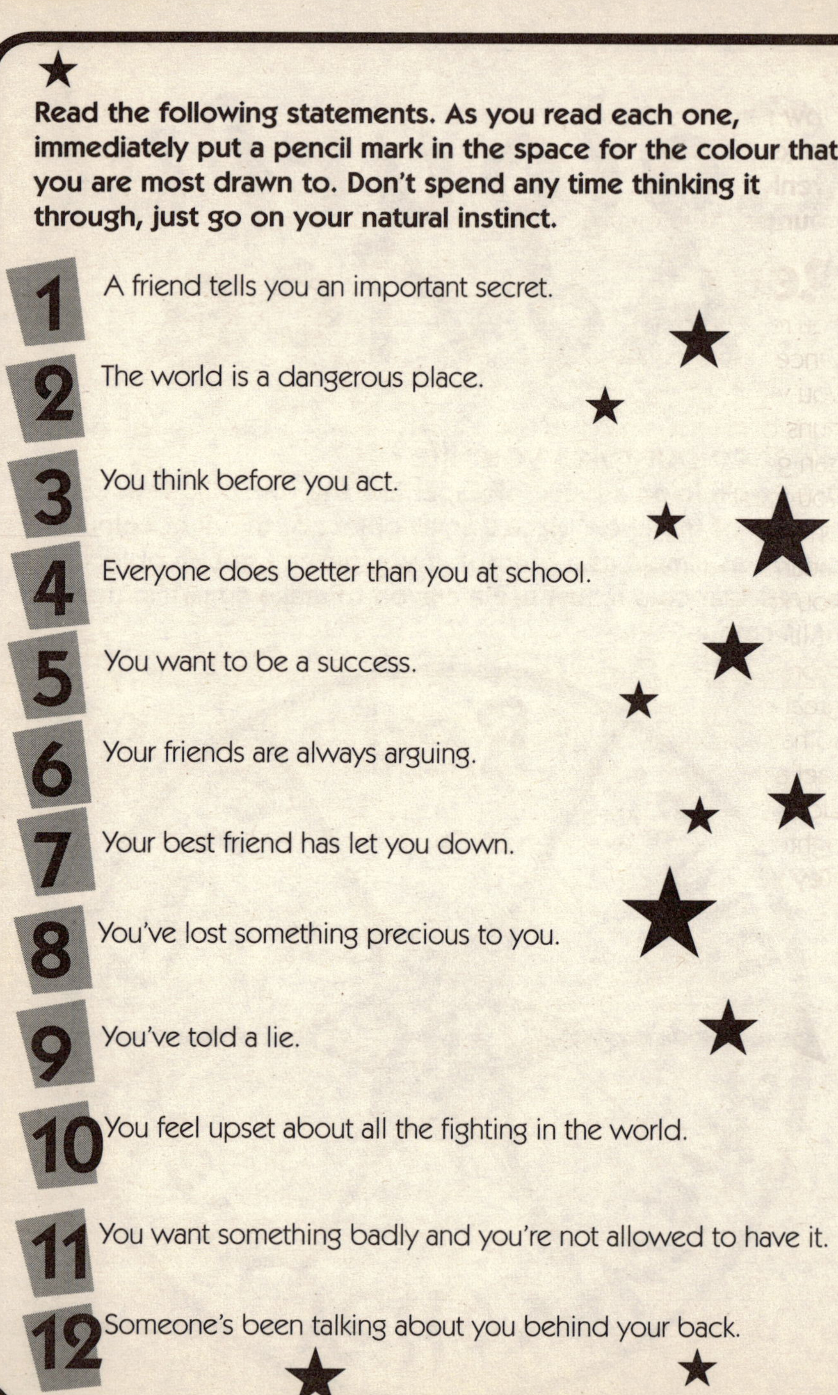

Read the following statements. As you read each one, immediately put a pencil mark in the space for the colour that you are most drawn to. Don't spend any time thinking it through, just go on your natural instinct.

1. A friend tells you an important secret.

2. The world is a dangerous place.

3. You think before you act.

4. Everyone does better than you at school.

5. You want to be a success.

6. Your friends are always arguing.

7. Your best friend has let you down.

8. You've lost something precious to you.

9. You've told a lie.

10. You feel upset about all the fighting in the world.

11. You want something badly and you're not allowed to have it.

12. Someone's been talking about you behind your back.

Now read the conclusion for the colour you have the most marks for. Don't worry if you have two or more colours pretty evenly matched. This just means that different elements of your personality are coming through strongly.

Red

You're very strong-minded. Once you know what it is that you want, you go for it with all guns blazing. Sometimes this can get you into hot water, as you trample over other people on the way. But you don't mean to upset anyone, it's just you know what you want out of life! You also have a very moral streak and so you're a great person for other people to have on their side. If you feel an injustice has been done, you won't rest until it's righted.

Key word: strong-minded

Green

You're a very practical person. You're good at organizing things and you like working to schedules and meeting deadlines. You can handle working under pressure and are good at juggling different things at the same time. You're a bit of a peace-maker among your friends, as you hate any sort of arguing and will do anything to help people get on. Every now and again you have a bit of a burn-out and can't be

bothered to do anything for a week or two, but it's never long before you're back on track and beavering away like a good 'un.
Key word: juggler

Black

You're a bit of a mystery girl. You don't like to give too much away at first but wait until you get to know people really well before you show them more of the real you. This can work against you, as you're actually quite sensitive on the inside and people often just think you're cold or stuck up, so you can find yourself getting hurt. Try letting a bit more of the real you out – after all, you're sensitive and artistic, and when you set your mind to it you can create a really warm and happy atmosphere around you.
Key word: sensitive

Yellow

Yes, yellow people are just about as sunny as the colour that rules their lives. You're a real people person. You're open-minded and enthusi-astic, and you make friends easily because you're such good fun to be around. You're always on the lookout for new experiences and love trying new

things. The only hitch in your colour scheme is that no one ever expects you to feel down – you're the one who cheers everyone up, after all – so when you are down, they expect you to snap out of it yourself. Luckily for you, you usually do!

Key word: cheerful

White

If you're going to do something, it has to be done absolutely perfectly. You just won't accept second best. You're ambitious in everything you do and want to be number one. You're very much led by your head and tend to let your heart take a back seat. You don't mind company, but you're more than happy by yourself too, and you can find it hard to open up enough to really let others in. Whatever you choose to do, you're sure to go far.

Key word: perfectionist

Blue

You're a little on the shy side. You'd rather have one or two really close friends than hang around in a noisy crowd. You're a bit of a romantic and can take life quite seriously. You take your time to get to know people, but when you do you are a very caring and loyal friend and would never let anyone down. And when you're on your own, there's nothing you like better than a lovely bit of peace and quiet!

Key word: shy

Face the Dilemma

OK, so you've found out loads about yourself already. Now let's see how you cope with the real nitty-gritty. When it comes to the tricky things in life, do you go for the ostrich approach or are you a fan of the big face-off? When confronted with a dilemma of conscience, do you know just what to do or do you flounder in fear of the consequences? Read on and find out!

1. You're round at Granny's and she's just been baking your most favourite biccies. But horror of horrors, they're not for you! She leaves them on the cooling rack and pops down to the shops. You're not supposed to touch them. Do you:

A. Leave them alone – Granny's made you plenty of biscuits in your time?

B. Rearrange them to aid the cooling and when one topples off and breaks, eat that? After all, Granny wouldn't want to give a damaged biscuit away, would she?

C. Scoff a couple really quickly before the guilt can set in, then rearrange them on the rack so that it looks like you've left them alone?

2. It's your turn to do the washing-up, which you hate. Do you:
A. Do it with good grace – it is your turn, after all?
B. Do it, but complain and grumble the whole way through, generally making everybody's lives miserable?
C. Negotiate a deal with your little brother to get him to do it? You promise to do it the next night – well, you'll cross that bridge when you come to it.

**3. Your sister's room is bang out of bounds, but you suspect she's got your brolly and it's raining, so …
Unfortunately, while hunting for your umbrella you knock over one of her china ornaments and break it. Do you:**

A. Calmly explain the circumstances around the incident and apologize profusely, while presenting her with an exact-matching brand-new ornament that you have bought to replace the one you broke?
B. Apologize sulkily? If she hadn't taken your umbrella …
C. Have a massive argument with her – it was her fault after all – end up not speaking to her for a week and finally apologize only because you want to borrow a CD from her.

4. You're round at your best friend's house. She's just gone to get you a drink when you spot her secret diary lying open on her desk. Do you:
A. Look away instantly – it's absolutely none of your business?
B. Fight with your conscience and lose, tiptoe over for a sneaky peak and then feel mortified as she's written loads of nice stuff about you and all you can do is betray her trust?
C. Go for a quick shufty, see what she's written about you and go into a huge sulk – apparently she's not sure she can trust you?

5. Your best mate's just had a new haircut and it looks good enough for Hallowe'en! She asks your opinion. Do you:
A. Come straight out with it, tell her it's awful and suggest she gets straight back to the salon and tells them to fix it now?
B. Try to change the subject and when that doesn't work tell her that you wouldn't wear your hair like that but as long as she's happy with it that's OK?
C. Tell her it looks absolutely gorgeous? She's obviously pleased with it and you don't want to upset her.

6. You've forgotten your games kit for the fifth week running. Do you:
A. Own up and accept that you're in your teacher's bad books again?
B. Feel so sick at the thought that you go completely grey and get sent home anyway?
C. Say, 'Well, miss, you're not going to believe this but there was a mini-hurricane in our street this morning and …'?

7. You're round at your friend's house and her dad is cooking you dinner. When he serves it up, it's the one thing you can't stand – peas! Do you say:
A. 'I'm really sorry but I'm afraid me and peas just don't see eye-to-eye. Do you mind if I leave mine?'
B. 'Peas … oh … er … my favourite!'?
C. 'I'm really sorry but I've got this terrible allergy. If I eat peas I go green and my head swells up to the size of a beach ball. It's pretty frightening to see, believe me!'?

8. There's a new girl in your class. It seems nearly everyone's decided she's stuck up, without really getting to know her, because she wears smart clothes and speaks a little differently. You feel a bit sorry for her. Do you:
A. Stride over to her and say, 'Hi' – it must be really tough being the new girl and you for one are going to give her a chance to fit in?
B. Make an effort to defend her when other people are talking

about her, but stop short of actually going to make friends? She
can always come to you if she wants.
C. Do nothing about it? She may be OK, but nobody else likes
her and you'd rather just go with the flow.

**9. Someone's been passing a naughty note around during
lessons. It lands in the hands of the teacher and no one
seems prepared to own up. Everyone's going to have to
stay in after school if the culprit isn't found. You think you
know who it is. Do you:**
A. Immediately put your hand up and announce in front of the
whole class that you know who's responsible?
B. Keep it to yourself – it was nothing to do with you and you
don't really want to get involved?
C. Confront the person in question at lunchtime and suggest they
own up? After all, you're sure it'll be better for them in the long
run if they're honest about it now.

**10. A friend of yours has confided in you that she's feeling
a bit low because her granny's unwell, but she doesn't**

**really want it to be common
knowledge. Later another
friend starts complaining to
you about your first friend,
saying she's a real misery guts
and is bringing everyone down.
Do you:**
A. Not mention your friend's
granny at all, but just mumble,
'Yeah, I know'? After all, it's more
important that you keep to yourself something told in confidence.
B. Hint at what's up, saying that
there may be reasons why your
friend's a bit sad at the moment
and perhaps your second friend
should bear that in mind?

C. Instantly explain the reason why your friend is being so miserable? You know it was told to you in confidence, but it's only fair that people know and then they can treat her accordingly.

Mainly 'A's: Honesty's Your Policy

Well, you've certainly decided that honesty's always the best path to follow. On the whole, you're right. In most situations it definitely is best to take the honest approach. But there's a little something known as diplomacy that might come in handy every now and again. Sometimes people are a little bit economical with the truth in order to spare other people's feelings or to prevent anyone being hurt. Being brutally frank can come across as a little on the abrupt side, and you don't really want to upset anyone, after all. You certainly know right from wrong, and that's something to be proud of, but remember that the odd half-truth, in the right circumstances, is no bad thing.

Key word: honest

Mainly 'B's: On the Fence

Oh dear, you don't like a dilemma at all, do you? If there's a problem you like to ignore it in the hope that it'll simply not be there next time you look! Sometimes this policy actually works, but in a lot of cases ignoring a problem simply makes it worse. You can be a bit of a worrier at the best of times, so getting things off your chest will definitely make you feel better all round. Facing up to things doesn't necessarily mean a confrontation, it just means taking a deep breath, speaking your mind and treating others in the way you would like to be treated yourself. Having said that, your passive policy means that you don't tread on many toes – you'd hate to hurt anyone's feelings – but watch out that you don't get trodden on yourself!

Key word: avoider

Mainly 'C's: Head First

Wow! You deal with everything at full throttle. You've got a bit of a hot head and sometimes open your mouth before your brain's properly in gear. You don't like being caught out or proved wrong, and you can stick up for yourself. You certainly know right from wrong, but you some-times just can't help trying to get yourself out of a tricky situation with a little white lie. Your hot-headedness can be a good thing, though, as you're not afraid to stand up and be counted when a friend needs your help. You're prepared to wade in and sort a situation out where others would fear to tread. But remember, if you stay cool and tell the truth, many of your tricky situations won't seem half so tricky after all.

Key word: headstrong

YOU MADE IT!

Congratulations!

You made it through, faced the facts and found out all there was to know about you-know-who! Don't forget to collect up your key words for your complete personality profile. Well done. Isn't it amazing what you can learn about yourself when you simply

Dare to Ask!